JOHN KNOX.

# JOHN KNOX:

## HIS IDEAS AND IDEALS

## JAMES STALKER, D.D.,

*Professor of Church History, United
Free College, Aberdeen*

## HODDER AND STOUGHTON

27, PATERNOSTER ROW

1904

*Printed by Hazell, Watson & Viney, Ld., London and Aylesbury.*

TO MY STUDENTS

# PREFACE

IN 1905 not only Scotland but her sons and daughters in distant lands will be celebrating, amidst the sympathy of the world, the Quatercentenary of the birth of the greatest of Scotsmen ; and this volume is offered as a contribution to this event. What has specially guided me, in addition to the interest of the occasion, has been the desire to make the Reformer's own sentiments better known. These are contained in volumes which are read by few ; and they are concealed beneath a repellent orthography ; but there is virtue in them which ought to be felt ; and I have endeavoured to release it. I do not pretend to have given a complete collection of Knox's good things ; but at least I have creamed them and furnished enough to familiarise the reader not only with his ideas but with the remarkable phraseology in which these were expressed ; and my hope is that the following pages may help to make it true that " he, being dead, yet speaketh."

Ample acknowledgments are due not only to the standard work of Dr. M'Crie and the solid volumes of Dr. Hume Brown, but also to the slighter sketches by Mrs. M'Cunn, Mr. Taylor Innes, and the late Dr. W. M. Taylor of New York, each of which has its own special charm. Upon *John Knox's House* and the translation into modern English of *The History of the Reformation* much affectionate and successful labour has been bestowed by Mr. Charles J. Guthrie. The lecture in Carlyle's *Heroes*, though brief, was epoch-making; there is a fine touch in the late R. W. Barbour's chapter in *The Evangelical Succession*; and R. L. Stevenson's essays in *Men and Books* is fresh and suggestive. But it is to Dr. David Laing's six volumes of *Knox's Works* that the reader must turn who desires to see Knox face to face; and it is to this conscientious editor's immortal labours that I have to express the deepest debt of gratitude.

ABERDEEN, 20 *October*, 1904.

# CONTENTS

## BOOK FIRST

### *JOHN KNOX*

#### CHAPTER I.

PAGE

EARLY YEARS . . . . . . . . . . 3


#### CHAPTER II.

EXILE . . . . . . . . . . . 25


#### CHAPTER III.

THE SCOTTISH REFORMATION . . . . . . 53


#### CHAPTER IV.

CLOSING YEARS . . . . . . . . . 82

# BOOK SECOND
## *HIS IDEAS*

### CHAPTER I.

HIS BOOKS . . . . . . . . . . 97

PAGE

### CHAPTER II.

HIS RELIGIOUS CONVICTIONS . . . . . . 122

### CHAPTER III.

HIS POLITICAL OPINIONS . . . . . . . 166

# BOOK THIRD
## *HIS IDEALS*

### CHAPTER I.

THE SCOTS CONFESSION OF FAITH . . . . . 193

### CHAPTER II.

THE BOOK OF COMMON ORDER . . . . . . 214

### CHAPTER III.

THE BOOK OF DISCIPLINE . . . . . . . 225

# BOOK FIRST

*JOHN KNOX*

# CHAPTER I.

## EARLY YEARS

JOHN KNOX was born at Haddington in the year 1505. Neither place nor date is, indeed, absolutely beyond dispute ; and the slight uncertainty has afforded ample room for the conflicts of antiquarians. The place may have been the village of Gifford, two or three miles from Haddington, but was more probably Gifford-gate, a portion of Haddington itself ; and the date may have been a few years later, even as much as ten years, as one keen investigator in such matters has recently suggested ; but the variations from the received date are less likely to have been due to exceptional knowledge and care than to carelessness, which in regard to such points was common in those days. Some people even in our day do not know the exact date of their own birth.

In the sixteenth century Haddington appears to have occupied a more outstanding position than it now does among the towns of Scotland, and, lying on the route of armies advancing from England, it had suffered much in the wars with which during the preceding centuries that part of the country was incessantly harassed. In Knox's time it contained two monasteries and an abbey; so that he had constantly before his eyes, in the years when impressions penetrate most deeply, the system of religion which he was destined to destroy; and, besides, there were several chapels and churches, one of which, on account of its prominence in the landscape, bore the title of the Lamp of Lothian. The town also possessed a school of note, in which, it may be presumed, the future reformer received the elements of education, as no fewer than three other Scottish worthies had done before him—Bower, Wyntoun and Major.

The name of Knox was not scarce in Scotland in that age, or confined to one district of the country; so that it is impossible to infer with any degree of certainty a connection with him every time it turns up in the records of the period. The most prominent Knoxes in the country were those of Ranfurly in Renfrewshire, but no connection between them and the Reformer has been established. In an interview with the Earl of Bothwell, who had estates in Haddingtonshire, Knox said, as he has himself recorded in his *History of the Reformation in Scotland* : " My grandfathers, paternal and maternal, and my father have served your lordship's predecessors, and some of them have died under their standards " ; [1] which appears to indicate that he was a farmer's son with an attachment to the soil and to the feudal superior. His father's name was William, as was also that of his brother, who figures here and there in his writings as a substantial merchant, trading in his own ship with England, and as a sincere adherent of the Reformed faith. His mother was a Sinclair—a name which he himself sometimes employed in signing his letters, when it was dangerous to make use of his own. Thus it will be seen that he belonged, by birth and upbringing, to the lower order of the middle class, which he was to do so much to educate and elevate ; although he was destined to be associated in a remarkable degree with the nobility of his native country ; while for the masses of the community, which in our day bulk so largely in the thoughts of religious leaders, he had, apart from his faith in the uplifting influences of the Gospel, very little of the sympathy of the democrat, his commonest name for this class being " the rascal multitude."

[1] *History*, ii. 343.

Of how Knox came to be set apart for the priesthood, whether by his own choice or by the desire of his parents, we have received no information. But, after being educated at the high-school of his native town, he entered the University of Glasgow in 1522, when he was seventeen years of age. As Haddington lay in the diocese of St. Andrews, it might have been expected that he would have connected himself with the university of that place ; but he may have been attracted to the city of the West by the fame of John Major, a Haddingtonshire man like himself and at that date the most renowned professor in the country. It is generally believed that Knox owed not a little to this teacher, especially in the formation of his political views, as did also George Buchanan, who was a student under the same professor a little later at St. Andrews, to which Major had been transferred. Although a bold and progressive thinker, Major never severed himself from the old Church. Buchanan became the foremost Humanist of his age in Scotland and won a European celebrity for the elegance of his Latinity. In this direction Knox achieved no special distinction. His scholarship never was worn as an ornament. But it was ample for the needs of the day, for which he employed it. He could refer with facility to the writings of the Fathers and to the incidents of Church History, so far as he needed them. He had of course the mastery of Latin, this being the language in which the intercourse of the learned was carried on and the instructions of universities delivered. Circumstances led to his familiar use of the French language. But, above all, he threw himself on the study of the Holy Bible, which he read in the original tongues, having acquired Hebrew when he was over forty. He was concerned in the translation of the Bible into English which goes by the name of the Geneva Version ; and it is from this that his own quotations are generally made ; these having for the modern reader, on this account, an odd and uncouth sound. It is in the use of his native tongue, however, that he is a master, his words being, in comparison with those of ordinary writers, like hail to rain, or like bullets in comparison with arrows. His spelling, which is very arbitrary, gives to his writings a foreign and repulsive look ; but, in reality, it is quite easy to read them ; and it is useless to continue printing them in the old orthography.

As has been remarked, it was in the year 1522, when he was seventeen years of age, that he entered the University of Glasgow. Thereafter he lived fifty years, dying in 1572. But for exactly the half of this period—namely, from 1522 to 1546 —we have next to no information about him; except that a document has been discovered in which he signs himself, in Latin, "John Knox, minister of the Sacred Altar, of the diocese of St. Andrews, notary by Papal Authority," which betokens that he had become a priest and employed himself, either occasionally or regularly, in notarial business, which would in our day be done by lawyers but in those days was included among the multifarious employments of the priesthood. When again he emerges into visibility, he is engaged in the work of tuition in a noble family in the neighbourhood of his birthplace. Such employment has always been among those in which men educated for the sacred office might be found engaged; but it is extraordinary to find Knox still occupied with it at the age of two-and-forty. This gives colour to the idea that the date of his birth is too early. But of course there may have been other reasons for the anomaly, such, for example, as scruples about engaging in the regular work of the priesthood. From the time when, in 1547, he comes clearly into view as a public character, we can follow him with full intelligence to the close of his life.

Indeed, his own writings, which abound with autobiographical material, continue from this point to the end without any considerable break. But the mind of the student of Knox lingers wistfully over the unrecorded interval between his seventeenth and his forty-second year. It reminds us of the long period of silence in the biography of our Lord, which is broken only by the incident of His first visit to Jerusalem. Though destitute of the delightful garrulity of Luther about himself, Knox is not particularly reticent; yet there are certain parts of his own biography where we cannot but keenly wish that he had told more; and this is one of them. We are left to infer back from his subsequent life, which is known, to this part, which is unknown.

Of one thing we may be certain, that he obtained in those years a precise and extensive knowledge of the religious system which it was to be the work of his life to pull down. Of this he always speaks in the most uncompromising terms, like one whose mind is made up and whose knowledge is so ample and detailed that it is of no use for anyone to argue with him. In Luther's mind we are permitted to see the doubts and hesitations of one who had been trained to venerate the authority and the institutions of the ancient faith and who, when first he began to perceive that he must oppose the traditional system, felt all the horror of a sacrilege. Those conflicts of his with the Devil, which excite so different emotions in different minds, were, in reality, only the imaginative equivalents of very real and just fears, haunting a private man, who was not only departing himself but leading multitudes away from the customs of the fathers, lest he should be leading them to their eternal ruin. Of such timidity there is in Knox no trace; and this may be due to the fact that he had had so long to observe and to think before he came forward as a public guide; though it may be also attributed to the fact mentioned by Dr. McCrie, whose statement has been censured as unpatriotic but never disproved, that the corruption of the Roman Catholic Church had reached a greater height in Scotland than in any other country of Europe. Knox always refers to the old Church as a system past redemption, in defence of which it is useless and impossible to speak. The secularity and rapacity of the higher clergy, who lived as nobles and occupied themselves with everything except religion; the numbers and the viciousness of the friars, who swarmed like locusts in the country and corrupted the morals of the population through the confessional, imperilling the purity of every household by the fury of their passions; the ignorance of the parish priests and their neglect of preaching, whilst they performed the routine of public worship in an unknown tongue—these and suchlike features of the actual condition of the Church were palpable and notorious, crying to Heaven for a reformation in root and branches.

In Luther's case we know the steps by which the Reformer himself was led into the light; and the affecting story belongs to the romance of Church History. But in the case of Knox we possess no such autobiographical details. On his deathbed he asked his wife to read to him the seventeenth chapter of St. John, " in which," said he, " I first cast anchor "; but, when this crisis took place, he did not indicate, and he has not indicated it in any of his writings. That there was a crisis there can, however, be little doubt; and the practised skill with which he deals with cases of spiritual upheaval in other souls suggests what had been its nature. In the account of his first preaching in Edinburgh in the year 1555 there is a singular little notice, which will be of significance in this respect to those who have any acquaintance with such matters. To himself it was evidently very notable; for he introduces this morsel of personal history at the very commencement of his

account of a great public movement. " At last came
John Knox in the end of the harvest, in the year of
God 1555, who, first being lodged in the house
of that notable man of God, James Syme, began
to exhort secretly in that same house ; whereto
repaired the Laird of Dun, David Forres, and some
certain personages of the town, among whom was
Elizabeth Adamson, then spouse of James Barron,
burgess of Edinburgh, who, by reason that she
had a troubled conscience, delighted much in the
company of the said John, because that he,
according to the grace given unto him, opened
more fully the fountain of God's mercies than did
the common sort of teachers that she had heard
before (for she had heard none except friars), and
did with such greediness drink thereof that at her
death she did express the fruit of her hearing to
the great comfort of all those that repaired to
her ; for, albeit that she suffered the most grievous
torment in her body, yet out of her mouth was
heard nothing but praising of God, except that
sometimes she would lament the troubles of those
that were troubled by her. Being sometimes demanded by her sisters what she thought of that
pain which she then suffered in her body, in respect
of that wherewith sometimes she was troubled in
spirit, she answered : ' A thousand years of this

torment, and ten times more joined unto it, is not to be compared to the quarter-of-an-hour that I suffered in my spirit. I thank my God through Jesus Christ, that has delivered me from that most fearful pain ; and welcome be this, even so long as it pleases His godly Majesty to exercise me therewith.' A little before her departure, she desired her sisters and some others that were beside her to sing a psalm ; and, among others, she appointed the ciii. Psalm, beginning, ' My soul, praise thou the Lord alway,' which ended, she said : ' At the teaching of this psalm began my soul first effectually to taste of the mercy of my God, which now to me is more sweet and precious than if all the kingdoms of the earth were given me to possess them a thousand years.' The priests urged her with their ceremonies and superstitions ; to whom she answered : ' Depart from me, ye sergeants of Satan ; for I have refused, and in your own presence do refuse, all your abominations. That which ye call your sacrament and Christ's body (as ye have deceived us to believe in times past) is nothing but an idol, and has nothing to do with the right institution of Jesus Christ ; and, therefore, in God's name, I command you not to trouble me.' They departed, alleging that she raved and wist not what she said. And she, shortly thereafter,

slept in the Lord Jesus, to the no small comfort of
those who saw her blessed departing. This we
could not omit of this worthy woman, who gave
so notable a confession, before that the great light
of God's Word did universally shine through this
realm." [1]    In scenes like this Knox was quite at
home ; in these the Reformation properly consisted,
although they are little heard of ; and Knox's
familiarity with them not only separates him by
the whole breadth of the heavens from the mere
ecclesiastic, who is concerned only with public
meetings and Church courts, but affords an interesting glimpse into his own spiritual history.

Knox was not, indeed, a reformer in the same
sense as Zwingli or Luther——men in whom the conception of a new Church and a new world arose as
an original inspiration and who fought their way
to clear apprehensions of the truth by the force
of their own spiritual genius. He belonged to
the second generation ; and his merit lay in the
thoroughness with which he grasped ideas which
were already in the air, in the force with which he
drove these into the mind of his country, and in
the institutions by which he provided for their conser-
vation. In the first book of his *History of the
Reformation*, he has himself lovingly commemorated

[1] *History*, i. 245.

those who were his predecessors. The stirrings of dissatisfaction with the actual condition of things and of aspiration after a better time came originally from England, as many as thirty persons of condition being tried for being followers of Wycliffe as early as 1494 in Ayrshire, which in the subsequent period remained a centre of reforming activity. Even before this, a spar from the wreck of the reforming efforts of Huss in Bohemia was thrown up on the East coast of Scotland, in the person of Paul Craw, a Bohemian physician, who was burnt to death at St. Andrews in 1431. As the Reformation blazed forth in Germany through the teaching of Luther, the sparks began to fall even in Scotland. " At this time," says Knox, "the knowledge of God did wondrously increase within this realm, partly by reading, partly by brotherly conference, which in those dangerous days was used to the comfort of many ; but chiefly by merchants and mariners, who, frequenting other countries, heard the true doctrine affirmed, and the vanity of the papistical religion openly rebuked ; among whom Dundee and Leith were principals." [1] The truth penetrated the cloisters, and its presence was suspected even in the court. When James V. died, in 1543, there was, in the pocket of his coat, a list

[1] *History*, i. 61.

of no fewer than a hundred—another report says, a hundred and sixty—persons, some of them belonging to the highest nobility of the realm, whom the ecclesiastical authorities accused of heresy and were urging the king to cut off.

But the two men, to whom, in the highest sense, the title of Reformer belongs in Scotland are undoubtedly Patrick Hamilton and George Wishart; and on both Knox bestows, in his *History*, ample and affectionate commemoration. The former of the two had learned the doctrines of the Reformation at the feet of Luther and Melanchthon themselves and, in imitation of the latter, whose principal theological work bears the name of *Common Places*—a term signifying heads or subjects under which the contents of a book are arranged—had given them to his countrymen in their native tongue in a brief volume popularly known as *Patrick's Places* and printed in full by Knox in the *History*. He had to die for his opinions at St. Andrews in 1527; but the charm of his youth and noble lineage, his sweetness of disposition, the cruelty of his martyrdom, and the constancy of his faith in the hour of death so penetrated the heart of the country with ruth and inquiry, that it was commonly said that the smoke [1] of Master Patrick had infected all

[1] "reek."

on whom it had blown. A striking evidence of the rapidity with which the new opinions were spreading was afforded by the passing of an Act of Parliament in 1543, giving permission to all to read the Scriptures in their own tongue and abolishing all acts to the contrary. "This," says Knox, "was no small victory of Christ Jesus, fighting against the conjured enemies of His verity. Then might have been seen the Bible lying on almost every gentleman's table. Thereby did the knowledge of God wondrously increase, and God gave His Holy Spirit to simple men in great abundance." [1]

But the most distinguished of the martyrs of the Reformation was George Wishart. Of his life Knox gives, in his *History*, an account that is classic in its condensed completeness. "A man," he calls him, "of such grace as before him was never heard within this realm, and are rare yet to be found in any man, notwithstanding this great light of God that since his days has shined unto us." He was brother of the Laird of Pitarrow, in Forfarshire, and first fell under the suspicion of the ecclesiastical authorities through teaching the Greek Testament in Montrose. The chief scene of his labours was Dundee, from which, however, he was

---

[1] *History*, i. 100.

banished through the machinations o the hierarchy. Passing to the West country, he received a hearty welcome there. But, hearing that the plague had broken out in Dundee, he returned ; and, preaching from the town-wall to the diseased on the one side and the healthy on the other, he exhibited such courage and intrepidity in grappling with the terrible visitation that he became the idol of the inhabitants, among whom the Reformation in subsequent years possessed a numerous following. Nevertheless, he was hounded from the place by the agents of the Church and had to flee to Edinburgh. The last place in which he preached was Haddington, Knox's native town. On 16 January 1546 he was arrested at the neighbouring House of Ormiston ; and on 1 March he suffered at the stake in St. Andrews.

The contriver of this judicial murder, as well as the instigator for many years of all the measures taken against the spread of the Reformed doctrines in the country, was Cardinal Beaton, the Primate of Scotland, who, surrounded by other proud prelates, lounged out of a window in his palace, to watch the sufferings of the martyr, after giving orders that all the guns of the Castle should be pointed to the place of execution, lest there should be any attempt at a rescue. This man was a typical ecclesiastic of the time. He was of noble family and had filled numerous political offices, as member of parliament, ambassador, and the like. On the death of James V., he produced a will of the deceased monarch, by which he was constituted Regent of the kingdom ; but his claims were set aside for those of the Earl of Arran, over whom, however, he soon acquired complete ascendency. Meantime he had been rising from stage to stage of ecclesiastical dignity, till, in 1538, he obtained the hat of a cardinal. He was a man of towering ambition and great energy, which was directed with special vigour towards clearing the Church of heresy. But his character was wholly unworthy of his sacred office : he was acknowledged to be the father of a number of sons and daughters, the latter of whom he married into the noble families of the country. When such was the record of the highest dignitary of the Scottish Church, what was to be expected of the rest of the clergy ? And this was the man who was hunting to death people as virtuous as he was vicious. Blunted as the conscience of the country had become through the long prevalence of such abuses, there were not awanting those now who were sensible of the glaring inconsistency ; and the martyrdom of Wishart wrought up their indignation to fever heat. They resolved that the murder of their beloved teacher should be avenged ; and five of them—not ignorant

fanatics, but all persons of repute, including Norman
Leslie, brother of the Earl of Rothes, and Kirkcaldy
of Grange—surprised the Cardinal in his own palace
on 29 May 1546 and stabbed him to death, after
assuring him that their only motive was to avenge
the death of Wishart and remove an obstinate
enemy of the holy Evangel.[1]   Of course they knew
themselves to be outlaws ; but they seized the
Castle of St. Andrews and defied the Government,
while there gathered round them a band bearing
some resemblance to that which gathered round
David in the Cave of Adullam, yet including
also such men as Henry Balnaves, a Lord of
Session, and Sir David Lindsay, the poet.   For
months they held out against all the power that the
Government was able to bring against them by
land ; but at length their stronghold was captured
by ships summoned by the Queen Regent from
France ; and in the same vessels the Castillians, as
they were called, were borne away to that country,
to be imprisoned there in fortresses or condemned
to the galleys.

It is in connection with these stirring events that
Knox emerges from the obscurity in which he had
been enveloped for five-and-twenty years.   When
Wishart came from Dundee to Eastlothian, Knox

[1] HERKLESS, *Cardinal Beaton.*

"waited upon him carefully," as he narrates himself; and he was with him during his activity in Haddington. It was at the house in which Knox was acting as tutor that the martyr was arrested; and Knox desired to accompany him; but the servant of God replied : " Nay, return to your pupils; [1] and God bless you! one is sufficient for a sacrifice." Unwillingly Knox yielded, giving up a two-handed sword which he had been bearing before the Reformer—a means of protection to which the latter had had to resort, and for the use of which, in spite of the unwarlike nature of his employments hitherto, Knox was not perhaps ill adapted.

But Knox was now a marked man, and the myrmidons of the hierarchy were on his track. At all events he felt himself insecure; and he betook himself to the Cave of Adullam at St. Andrews. The parents of his pupils were also suspected persons; and, either for this reason or because they put a high value on the instructions of their tutor, they permitted their boys to accompany him. " Besides their grammar and other human authors," says Knox, speaking of himself, " he read unto them a catechism, account whereof he caused them to give publicly in the parish Church of St. Andrews. He read, moreover, unto them the Evangel of John,

[1] "bairns."

proceeding where he left off at his departing from
Longniddry, where before his residence was ; and
that lecture he read in the chapel within the Castle
at a certain hour." [1]  By these prelections the
attention of the Castillians was directed to the
gifted newcomer ; and they began to urge him
to favour them with the exercise of his talents
in the pulpit.  But to this he was entirely averse,
till, instigated by Sir David Lindsay, they resorted
to a pious ruse to overcome his scruples.  One
Sunday their preacher, John Rough, after dis-
coursing on the election of ministers, there and
then addressed to Knox a call in the name of all
present, proceeding in these moving terms : " In
the name of God and of His Son Jesus Christ,
and in the name of those here present who call
you by my mouth, I charge you that ye refuse
not this holy vocation, but that you tender the
glory of God, the increase of Christ's kingdom,
the edification of your brethren, and the comfort
of me, whom you understand well enough to be
oppressed with the multitude of labours, that you
take upon you the public office and charge of
preaching, even as you look to avoid God's heavy
displeasure and desire that He shall multiply His

---

[1] *History*, i. 186.

graces with you." Then, addressing himself to the
congregation, he demanded, "Was not this your
charge to me? and do you not approve this vocation?" They answered: "It was; and we approve
it." Abashed and terrified, Knox fled to his
chamber, as Saul, in similar circumstances, hid
himself among the stuff. For days his distress
continued; but, when he came forth from his
privacy and ascended the pulpit, it was to deliver
a sermon which made all who heard it aware that
a prophet had risen up amongst them. Some of
the listeners said: "Others lop off the branches of
the papacy, but he strikes at the root, to destroy
the whole"; others said: "If the doctors and
*magistri nostri* defend not now the Pope and
his authority which in their own presence is so
manifestly impugned, the Devil have my part of
him and of his laws likewise"; others said: "Master
George Wishart spoke never so plainly, and yet
he was burnt; even so will he be." [1] Thus were
the lips unsealed which had been kept dumb so
long and the sluices opened to let out the waters
of thought and conviction which had so long been
accumulating. In the weeks that followed there
began to blossom in the heart of Knox that peculiar

[1] *History*, i. 192.

affection which knits the minister of the Gospel to those for whom he has travailed in birth till Christ be formed in them ; and to the end of his life he cherished towards St. Andrews that first love which a pastor feels for the first place in which he has exercised his ministry.

## CHAPTER II.

### EXILE

WHEN the garrison of St. Andrews had to surrender, Knox, like the rest of the Castillians, was carried off to captivity in France ; and it was his hard lot to be sent to the galleys. These things took place in 1547, when he was two-and-forty years of age. He was a man rather under the middle height, with broad shoulders, swarthy face, black hair, and a beard of the same colour a span-and-a-half long. He had heavy eyebrows, beneath which the eyes were deeply sunk, while the cheekbones were prominent and the cheeks ruddy. The mouth was large, and the lips full, especially the upper one. The whole aspect of the man was not unpleasing ; and, in moments of emotion, it was invested with an air of dignity and majesty. So he is described by a contemporary, writing carefully for the purpose of instructing an engraver engaged on a portrait of the subject. The late Thomas Carlyle, in an

essay which he wrote in old age on the portraits
of Knox, expressed strong scepticism as to the
accuracy of the traditional bearded portraits, as
being too sensational, his preference being given,
on internal grounds, to what is known as the
Somerville Portrait, which is that of an extremely
Scotch, sensible, good-humoured, but beardless face.
It has, however, since been proved by Dr. Hume
Brown, through the recovery of the document above
quoted, that the traditional portrait is the genuine one.[1]
The face is more that of a French or Swiss pastor
than of an ordinary Scot ; and the copious beard
supplies a feature which in any age must have
been peculiar.    After the date at which Knox
entered so dramatically—holding the two-handed
sword in front of Wishart—on the stage of public
life, he was to live other five-and-twenty years ;
and this period falls into two halves of almost
equal length—the first from 1547 to 1559, during
which he was out of his native country, save for
one somewhat prolonged visit in 1555-6, and the
second from 1559 to his death in 1572, during
which he was hardly ever out of Scotland and
never out of the island of Britain.

His twelve years of exile commenced with about

[1] HUME BROWN, *John Knox*, ii. 320.

a year-and-a-half in the French galleys, where he was the companion of convicts, and the whip of the slave-driver cracked over his head. The galley in which he was confined, *Nostre Dame* by name, sailed on the rivers of France, and, in addition to the hardness of their toil, the victims of justice were galled by its uselessness. Dr. Hume Brown has drawn, from official sources, a picture of the life of the galley–slaves appalling in its realism ; but there is room to hope that, in Knox's case at least, there may have been some mitigation of its horrors ; for during this time he edited, annotated and sent home to the friends of the Reformation in Scotland a treatise which a fellow-prisoner, Henry Balnaves, already mentioned, had written in the prison of Rouen ; and such literary activity would hardly have been compatible with a rigour of discipline as unmitigated as Dr. Hume Brown assumes to have prevailed. Knox tells a story of a priest, who ministered to the prisoners, carrying round, on one of the festivals of the Church, the image of some saint, to be kissed ; whereupon one of the prisoners stoutly refused and, when the holy man insisted, seized the painted piece of wood and, flinging it overboard, exclaimed : " Let us see if she can swim ; she is light enough." Of this adventure Knox is generally supposed to have been himself the hero ; but, if so, the fact that such an act of insubordination could be performed with impunity seems to indicate that the discipline was not very rigorous. Another sign of lax discipline is that four of the Castillians managed to escape from Mont St. Michel ; and it is an indication of the position held by Knox among his fellow-exiles that, before carrying out their design, they consulted him as to its lawfulness. His reply was that, if they could escape without shedding any man's blood, the attempt might lawfully be made. And made it was with success ; but so many vicissitudes had the runaways to encounter that Knox was in England before them. On one occasion the galley in which he was chained happened to sail round Scotland ; and it passed so near to the Fife coast that the spires of St. Andrews could be seen in the distance. Knox happened at the time to be so ill that his recovery was despaired of ; but, when a comrade pointing towards the land, asked him if he recognised it, " Yes," replied the invalid, raising himself on his elbow, " I know it well ; for I see the steeple of that place where God first in public opened my mouth to His glory ; and I am fully persuaded, how weak soever I now appear, that I shall not depart this life, till that my tongue shall glorify His godly name in the same place." This prophecy was destined to be remarkably fulfilled ; and it was only one of many instances which caused the character of seer or prophet to be attributed to Knox, both by others and himself, as it had previously been to Wishart and was afterwards to Peden and others of the Scots Worthies. The comrade who succoured Knox on this occasion was James Balfour, who lived to be Lord President in his native country, but became to Knox an object of abhorrence, because he appeared to him to have become a backslider from the faith and profession of his youth ; and this was not the only one of the Castillians who subsequently rose high in the world but, in the course of so doing, lost the ardour of his youthful convictions.

Such are the fragmentary notices which can be gleaned from this painful portion of Knox's life. In subsequent years he did not like to speak of it ; the iron had entered too deeply into his soul. Nevertheless he derived from it one invaluable lesson ; for it taught him to pray. In *A Declaration of the True Nature and Object of Prayer*—one of the tenderest things he ever wrote—he observes : "Trouble and fear are very spurs to prayer ; for, when man, compassed about with vehement calamities and vexed with continual solicitude, having by help of man no hope of deliverance, with sore oppressed and punished heart, fearing also greater punishment to follow, from the deep pit of tribulation doth call to God for comfort and help, such prayer ascendeth to God's presence and returneth not in vain. For I, the writer hereof, (let this be said to the laud and praise of God alone) in anguish of mind and vehement tribulation and affliction called to the Lord, when not only the ungodly but even my faithful brethren, yea, and my own self judged my cause to be irremediable. And yet in my greatest calamity, and when my pains were most cruel, would His eternal wisdom that my hands should write far contrary to the judgment of carnal reason, which His mercy hath proved true, blessed be His name! And, therefore, dare I be bold, in the verity of God's Word, to promise that, notwithstanding the vehemency of trouble, the long continuance thereof, the desperation of all men, the fearfulness, danger, dolour and anguish of our own hearts, if we call constantly to God, that beyond expectation of all men, He shall deliver ! " although he adds, with touching brevity, a little later : " How hard this battle is, no man knoweth but he who in himself hath suffered trial." [1]

So shy is he of speech on the subject of his

[1] *Works*, iii. 90, 100.

imprisonment that he has not informed us how
it came to an end. But in February 1549 he
was in England; and all the Castillians had also
been set free. At that date King Edward VI.
had already been for two years on the throne
of England; and under his godly encouragement
the work of reformation, which had proceeded
so slowly and dubiously during the reign of his
father, was going on apace. At the head of
ecclesiastical affairs was Cranmer, whose views were
broad and statesmanlike. The Church of England
had not then taken up the isolated position which
it has since adopted among the Churches of the
Reformation, but frankly recognised its unity with
all branches of the Church which had separated
from Rome; and Archbishop Cranmer did not
scruple to lay hold of men of talent, professing
the Reformed opinions, wherever he could find them,
and to send them forth as labourers into the harvest,
the harvest being truly great and the labourers
few. From the Continental Churches he introduced
professors to the theological chairs in the universities; and he was only too glad to secure for the
pulpit a preacher of the calibre of Knox from the
Scottish Church. Accordingly Knox found immediate
employment; and he continued in the service
of the Church of England for the next five

years.[1] No question about his orders was ever
raised ; his ability to do the work was the only
qualification needed ; for the spirit of power and of
love and of a sound mind was then breathing
over the Churches of the Reformation from end
to end, imparting to them a catholicity very different
from the sentiment which has sometimes since
borne that name falsely, because its purpose is to
exclude and not to include.

He was employed first at Berwick and subsequently at Newcastle-on-Tyne ; and he could afterwards say of his ministry there : " God is witness,
and I refuse not your own judgments, how simply
and uprightly I conversed and walked amongst you.
Though in His presence I am nothing but a mass
of corruption, rebellion and hypocrisy, yet, as concerning you and the doctrine taught amongst you,
as then I walked, so now do I write in the presence
of Him who only knoweth and shall reveal the
secrets of all hearts, that neither for fear did I spare
to speak the simple truth to you, neither for hope
of worldly promotion, dignity or honour did I
willingly adulterate any part of God's Scripture,
whether it were in exposition, in preaching, contention or writing, but that simply and plainly, as it
pleased the merciful goodness of God to give unto

[1] LORIMER : *John Knox and the Church of England.*

me the utterance, understanding and spirit, I did distribute the bread of life (I mean God's most holy Word) as of Christ Jesus I had received it. I sought neither pre-eminence, glory nor riches. My honour was that Christ Jesus should reign, my glory that the light of His truth should shine in you, and my greatest riches that in the same ye should be constant." [1]

But higher promotion was in store for him. In 1551 he was appointed one of the six Chaplains-in-Ordinary to the King, of whom two in turn should always be resident at court, while the other four, when not thus employed, were to itinerate in destitute parts of the country. Thus it fell to Knox's lot to be preacher to the most distinguished and influential audience in England ; and this position involved him in delicate operations, which were at that time in course of being performed. Thus, in 1552 he had a hand in the compilation of the Book of Common Prayer ; and he is known to have procured the insertion of a rubric explaining that by the act of kneeling at the reception of the sacrament no adoration of the elements is intended, " for that were idolatry, to be abhorred of all faithful Christians." " A runnagate Scot," complained a controversialist in the reign of Mary Tudor, " did take away the

[1] *Works*, iii. 165.

adoration or worshipping of Christ in the sacrament;
so much prevailed that one man's authority at
that time." In like manner an edition of the
Articles of the Church of England, issued in this
reign, was delivered to the six Royal Chaplains, of
whom Knox was one, to make a report of their
opinion touching the same, and, although nothing
can be pointed out in the Articles which indubitably
came from his hand, he was not the man to let
such an opportunity pass without making the most
of it.

If he did not remain in the Church of England,
it was not because that body was unwilling to
retain him, but because he was unwilling to commit
himself unreservedly to it. His appointment to the
See of Rochester is known to have been discussed
in the highest quarters, and it was probably due to
his own disinclination that it did not take place.
At all events it is certain that he was offered the
living of All Hallows, in Bread Street, London.
Indeed, his refusal of this preferment caused him
to be called before the Privy Council, where were
present the Bishops of Canterbury and Ely, my Lord
Treasurer, the Marquis of Northampton, the Earl of
Bedford, the Earl of Shrewsbury, Master Comptroller,
my Lord Chamberlain, both the Secretaries, and other
inferior Lords. He was asked three questions—why

he refused the benefice provided for him ; whether
he thought that no Christian might serve in the
ecclesiastical ministration according to the rites
and laws of the realm of England ; and whether
kneeling at the Lord's Table was not indifferent.
To the first he answered that he could be of more
use elsewhere than in London ; to the second, that
many things were worthy of reformation in the
ministry of England, without the reformation whereof
no minister did discharge or could discharge his
conscience before God ; for no minister in England
had authority to divide the lepers from the sound,
though this was a chief point of his office ; yet
did he not refuse such office as might appear to
promote God's glory in utterance of Christ's Gospel
in a mean degree, where more he might edify by
preaching of the true Word than hinder by suffer-
ance of manifest iniquity, seeing that reformation of
manners did not appertain to all ministers. To
the third he answered, that Christ's action in itself
was most perfect, and Christ's action was done
without kneeling ; that kneeling was man's addition
or imagination ; that it was most sure to follow
the example of Christ, whose action was done sitting
and not kneeling. It is strange to think of such
principalities and powers listening to such replies
or asking such questions. Yet, after long reasoning,

it was said unto him, that he was not called of any evil mind ; they were sorry to know him of a contrary mind to the Common Order. He answered that he was more sorry that a Common Order should be contrary to Christ's institution. With some gentle speeches he was dismissed.[1] But he continued after this to discharge his functions as before ; and we find him itinerating, not only in the North, but in Buckinghamshire and Kent.

Of Edward VI. Knox had formed the very highest opinion. " We had," says he, " a king of so godly disposition towards virtue and the truth of God, that none from the beginning passed him, and to my knowledge, none of his years did ever match him." But of the courtiers and statesmen by whom the youthful monarch was surrounded his estimate was very different ; and he prophesied distinctly what a backsliding there was likely to be in England, if a Romanist should come to the throne and the wind of persecution begin to blow upon the religion which had sprung up like the gourd of Jonah in the sunshine of the court. Already Knox had acquired the habit, of which no injunctions to the contrary could ever cure him, of introducing into his sermons allusions of the most uncompromising character to current events. In the very last sermon

[1] *Works*, iii. 87.

which he preached before the King, taking for his text
the words, " He that eateth bread with me hath lifted
up his heel against me," he proceeded to observe
that commonly the most godly princes had officers
and chief councillors most ungodly. Were David
and Hezekiah, he asked, princes of great and godly
gifts and experience, abused by crafty councillors
and dissembling hypocrites ? " What wonder is it,
then, that a young and innocent King be deceived
by crafty, covetous, wicked and ungodly councillors ?
I am greatly afraid that Achitophel be councillor,
that Judas bear the purse, and that Shebna be scribe,
comptroller, and treasurer." [1]  And there could be
no doubt to which persons in the auditory these
terms applied.

In July 1553 the precocious but delicate monarch
sank into the grave ; and, the following month, his
sister Mary came to the throne. A few months of
grace were allowed to the Protestants ; but, before
the end of the year, the Roman Catholic reaction
had set in with irresistible force ; and it was
dangerous for prominent professors of the Reformed
religion to be seen on the soil of England. Knox
lingered as long as he dared, still prosecuting the
work of preaching the Gospel after the time of
grace had expired ; and he went out of the country

[1] *Works*, iii. 282

only with compunction ; but at length the per-
suasions of his friends prevailed ; and in March
1554 he found himself at Dieppe, facing a new
period of exile on the Continent, which was to last
as long as the reign of the Queen.

He had no place to go to ; and, in spite of
his incessant labours in the service of the Church
of England, he was so poor that he was under the
necessity of appealing almost immediately to private
friends in England for the means of procuring daily
bread. After some uncertain movements from place
to place, in the course of which he came into personal
relations with several eminent Continental Reformers,
he arrived in Geneva, where he had the privilege of
forming the acquaintance of Calvin, then near the
height of his influence. By his advice he accepted
an invitation to become the pastor, or rather one
of the pastors, of the English congregation at
Frankfort-on-the-Main ; and in this position he was
settled before the end of the year.

This English congregation in a foreign city was
composed of exiles and their families, who had fled
from England to escape from the persecution of the
reigning monarch. Settlements of similar character
had at the same time been formed at other places
on the Continent, such as Zurich and Strasbourg ;

but Frankfort proved the favourite place of resort, because the use of a church had been granted to the exiles by the magistrates. The use of the same building had been previously obtained by a Walloon congregation, which had fled from England on the accession of Mary, and to the English the privilege was granted on condition that they employed the service of this French congregation—a condition which was understood to be sufficiently fulfilled by the employment of the English Prayer Book, with the litany and the responses left out and a few other slight modifications introduced. Such alterations suited Knox well enough, the portions left out being precisely those to which he had already in England expressed conscientious objections; and there were other persons in the congregation to whom this modified Prayer Book was more acceptable than the original.

On the other hand, there was a party who would have preferred the book unaltered. All, however, was going with tolerable smoothness, till a further party of exiles from England arrived on the scene, certain aggressive members of which, the first Sunday they were in church, gave the responses at the points at which they had been accustomed to do so in England; and, the following Sunday, they contrived to have the litany read. Knox, in

preaching, represented to them the disorderliness
of their conduct in interfering with an arrangement
agreed to before their arrival and laid down by
the magistrates as the condition on which the use
of the church had been allowed. But there was
an element in the congregation favourable to the
Prayer Book as it was ; and the newcomers carried
things with a high hand. They were not yet, indeed,
members of the congregation, and, by keeping them
out, Knox might have had a majority favourable
to his own views. He, however, disdained to make
use of this advantage ; and they were no sooner
in the majority than they proceeded to use their
strength against him and his supporters. Then
ensued a storm in a teapot, the minute details of
which are still traceable, if it were worth while ;[1]
and it has been said that the contest was the entire
Puritan Period in miniature. In the end Knox's
opponents resorted to the use of an equivocal
measure by which the controversy was ended as
far as he was concerned : carrying to the magistrates
a copy of a pamphlet which he had recently
published, entitled *A Faithful Admonition to
England*, they pointed out several references to the
Queen of England and to her husband, Philip of
Spain, of a character so unparliamentary that the

[1] *Works*, iv. 1 ff.

City of Frankfort might, it was suggested, become obnoxious to these potentates, if it was known to be harbouring the man who had made them. This device was successful, the magistrates requesting Knox to quit the city.

He returned to Geneva ; and with him went such of those who had been on his side in the controversy as were in a position to change their residence. By these was formed at Geneva a refugee congregation, which grew till it numbered over two hundred members. Of this body Knox became pastor, or rather one of the pastors ; for he had as colleague Christopher Goodman, who was to be closely associated with him in more phases than one of his subsequent history. Hardly had Knox, however, commenced his labours in this new sphere when he was called away to visit his native country, in which he stayed from September 1555 to July 1556.

Six years had elapsed since he had left Scotland ; and in the interval events had been marching at a rate of which Knox himself had had no conception ; the result being that he received a welcome far beyond his expectations. Partly the change was due to the growing intelligence of the country and to the utter inability of the Catholic Church, as it

then existed, to stand the least inquiry. Of this a
pathetic proof had been given in the year in which
Knox had left the country, when a Provincial Synod
passed no fewer than sixty-eight statutes of a re-
formatory character, in which it was confessed that
the root and cause of the troubles and heresies
which afflicted the Church were the corruption, the
profane lewdness, the gross ignorance of churchmen
of almost all ranks, particulars being added too un-
savoury for quotation. Partly it was due to the
influx into Scotland, on the accession of Mary in
England, of Protestants who might hope for less
inquisition there into their beliefs ; among whom
were such ministers as Harlaw and Willock, who
became extremely useful in the North. From
Edinburgh, on 9 November, Knox writes : " Albeit
my journey toward Scotland was most contrary
to my own judgment, yet this day I praise God
for them whom he made the instrument to draw
me from the den of my own ease, to contemplate
and behold the fervent thirst of our brethren,
night and day sobbing and groaning for the bread
of life. If I had not seen it with mine eyes in my
own country, I could not have believed it." And a
little later he writes : " The trumpet blew the old
sound three days together, till private houses of indifferent largeness could not contain the voice of it.

Oh, sweet were the death that should follow such forty days in Edinburgh as here I have had three!" It is not to be forgotten that Knox returned to his native land surrounded with a halo of prestige due to his association with the leaders of thought and action in other countries; but more is required to explain a success like this.

Among his hearers in Edinburgh were many solid and excellent citizens, the names of some of whom he gives, though they are now forgotten, and honourable women not a few. Of figures more notable were young Maitland of Lethington, whose subsequent course was to be so ambiguous, and Erskine of Dun, who was always faithful and continued throughout the subsequent years to be an ornament to the cause to which he was attached. By the latter Knox was taken to his residence in Forfarshire, where he entered into the labours of his predecessor Wishart with much success. Later his headquarters were at Calder House, near Midcalder, where not only did Sir James Calder and his sons espouse the cause, but round the preacher were gathered young men destined to rise to positions of the greatest influence in their native country— Lord Erskine, the future Earl of Mar ; Lord Lorn, afterwards Earl of Argyle ; and Lord James Stewart, afterwards the Regent Moray. From here he passed to Ayrshire and Lanarkshire, where the ground had been prepared by the Lollards of Kyle, already mentioned ; and here, among other men of distinction, the Earl of Glencairn joined him, proving to be of inestimable value to the cause in subsequent years. By Glencairn another great noble, the Earl Marischal, was brought into contact with Knox, whom he persuaded to write a letter to the Queen Regent ; for they were at the stage when young converts believe that the truth has only to be set forth in its naked simplicity to win universal assent. Knox penned the letter, putting into it not only the pith of his reasoning power but the utmost courtesy of which he was capable. But they were to learn the lesson that Old Adam is too strong for young Melanchthon ; for Mary of Lorraine, having perused it, handed it to the Archbishop of Glasgow, who was standing by, with the remark : " Please you, my lord, to read a pasquil "—a remark which, when Knox heard of it, entered like iron into his soul.

Thus was Knox permitted for months to go unchallenged up and down the country, by the attraction of his personality and the persuasion of his preaching winning adherents of great weight and in surprising numbers to the cause. But at length the sleeping enemy awoke ; and he was summoned to answer for himself in the Church of the Blackfriars in Edinburgh. Though well aware that the fate of Patrick Hamilton and George Wishart was probably in store for him, he answered the summons, appearing at the appointed day and hour. But the opposite party took fright and deserted the diet; whereupon he went on preaching in Edinburgh to still larger audiences. But the situation could not have lasted much longer as it was; and it was well that, at the critical juncture, he received a summons, which he did not feel himself entitled to disobey, to return to his charge at Geneva.

The value of this visit to his native country had been incalculable. The men and women whom he was privileged to bring to decision proved to be those on whom the whole weight of the cause was subsequently to rest, and they felt for him the affection and devotion due to the man to whom they owed themselves. Wherever he had gone, he had dispensed the Lord's Supper in the simple form of the Reformed Church; and people, long accustomed to the wearisome celebration of the Mass in a strange tongue, felt the charm of the unadorned function and entered into the communion of saints. He strongly dissuaded them from attending Mass; and, from this time forward, this became the mark of thorough and entire religious decision. He did not, however, merely enjoin this, but argued the question out with such disputants as Maitland of Lethington, so that they might have a reason in themselves for the line of conduct they pursued. He left behind him directions for conducting the devotional meetings in which they were to search the Scriptures and edify one another. He was even implored by the female portion of his adherents to guide them as to the garments it would be proper for women professing godliness to wear ; and this responsibility he did not decline, his opinion on this ticklish subject being still accessible.[1]

There had been another reason for this visit of Knox to his native country besides the public one. While engaged as a preacher in Northumberland five years before, he had formed the acquaintance of the family of Richard Bowes, Captain of Norham Castle. With this man's wife, who was the daughter of Roger Aske, of Aske in Yorkshire, he had formed a close intimacy, acting to her as spiritual guide, she being of a rare intelligence but of a scrupulous conscience and, for this reason, making constant demands upon the sympathy of her friend, who responded to them in a correspondence which forms one of the most characteristic

[1] *Works*, iv. 225 ff.

portions of his literary legacy. In the course of his intercourse with the mother, he formed an attachment for her daughter Marjory ; and, in spite of the opposition of her father and some other members of the family, they were engaged to be married before he left England ; and now, as he quitted Scotland, to return to Geneva, they were wedded ; and he took back with him not her only but Mrs. Bowes as well. This event in Knox's life did not cause the same amount of scandal as did the marriage of Martin Luther, the world having become accustomed to the spectacle of the marriage of men who had once, as priests or friars, taken the vow of celibacy. He was to give more cause for the derision of the profane when, Marjory Bowes having died in 1560, he married again in 1564, at the age of fifty-nine, his bride being a girl of sixteen or seventeen. By his first wife he had two sons, one of whom became a clergyman in the Church of England, and by the second three daughters, one of whom became the heroic Mrs. Welsh of Ayr.

For the next three years Knox was minister of the English congregation of Geneva ; and this was the most tranquil period of his life. Of the sublime scenery of the Alps he never, indeed, says a word ; but such silence was the custom of the age ; and he must have felt the influences of nature whether he was conscious of them or not. Of other advantages of his place of abode he was well aware. " I neither fear," he remarks, " nor ashame to say that Geneva is the most perfect school of Christ that ever was in the earth since the days of the Apostles. In other places I confess Christ to be truly preached ; but manners and religion so truly reformed I have not yet seen in any other place." [1] Such was the result of the vision of a city of God on earth which had formed itself in the mind of Calvin and of the force of will with which that great man had impressed his own ideas on the minds of his fellow-citizens. Knox, along with his colleague Goodman, was admitted to citizenship in 1558. Of actual intercourse of his own with Calvin we have comparatively little record ; but the two were so near of kin in spirit and aims that their fellowship must have been close and cordial ; and it is delightful to think of these two pacing the margin of the lovely Lake, absorbed in conversation on the highest themes. Though the elder of the two, Knox always speaks with veneration of his friend, as " that singular instrument of Christ Jesus in the glory of His

[1] *Works*, iv. 240.

Gospel." " From him," he adds, " we must confess, except that we would, in concealing the truth, declare ourselves to be unthankful, that we all have received comfort, light and erudition." [1] Of other persons of culture the city at that time contained not a few ; such, for example, as those who were engaged in translating the Geneva Bible ; and in Knox's own congregation there were persons of honour, quality and estate, many of them divines and students of divinity, besides merchants, trades-men and husbandmen.

In intercourse with friends like these his mind was stimulated, and he had leisure both to read and think. Hence it is not surprising that it is to these three years that the fullest statements of his opinions, both theological and political, belong. His longest theological production, a treatise on Predestination, was a task imposed on him by the divines with whom he was associated at Geneva, and it was sanctioned by the authorities of that city. The discussion of the subject of which it treated had waxed hot in Switzerland a little earlier ; and the author of the English work which Knox was appointed to answer had borrowed his arguments from the opponents of Calvin in that country—Servetus, Bolsec and Castellio. The most

[1] *Works*, v. 169.

notorious political treatise of Knox, on the contrary, *The Monstrous Regiment of Women*, was written without consultation with Calvin, and was vigorously repudiated by that divine, when it became apparent how much it was fitted to injure the cause of the Reformation. It was directed against Mary of Lorraine and Bloody Mary; but the latter died immediately after its publication; and Elizabeth, who succeeded, though a Protestant, disliked not only the book itself but the man who had written it, and the city from which it had been issued, almost as much as Mary, had she lived, could have done.

It was actually written at Dieppe, where Knox had arrived in 1557, intending to proceed to Scotland, from which an invitation to return had reached him, signed by several of the most influential of the adherents of the Reformation. But they changed their minds and intercepted him with an order not to come any further, the time being not yet ripe. For weeks he stayed with impatience in the seaport, waiting for further orders; while he waited, the fire burned, and he threw off this unfortunate pamphlet, to relieve his feelings. It brought him subsequently a world of trouble, and he had to try to explain it away both to Queen Elizabeth and Mary Queen of Scots; but as to the main positions of the book he died impenitent.

It is more pleasant to remember that during the weeks he stayed at Dieppe he preached in the town and may almost be called the founder of the vigorous Protestant Church which subsequently flourished there. He also visited, before returning to Geneva, Rochelle and other Protestant centres in the West of France. Indeed, he was thoroughly familiar with the condition of the French Church, and he translated into English an official account, which the Huguenots had issued, of a cruel massacre of which they had been the victims in Paris. We may close this section of his life with a moving story from this little-known document, or rather from an editorial addition, made by Knox himself: "Among others, God now of late days hath so triumphed in the death of a tender child of sixteen years of age, that the very blind people are compelled to confess that the mighty power of God worketh above nature with the sufferers, and openly fighteth against our enemies. This young gentleman, condemned to be burnt quick, was laid upon a manner of a wheel[1] above the fire, his face upward; but, as God's good pleasure and providence was, his tongue was not cut out, but a great piece of wood was put in his mouth, bound with a cord behind his neck. When the fire had so long burnt that

[1] "rowe."

the cord was consumed, and so the stick fell forth of his mouth, he began, when no life appeared to have remained, most comfortably to sing the Fortieth Psalm of David, having this beginning : ' Patiently have I abidden the Lord, who is eternal, and He hath inclined Himself unto me and hath heard my cry. He hath delivered me from the horrible pit, yea, from the pit of dolour, and hath placed my feet upon a sure rock. He hath put a new song in my mouth, yea, a thanksgiving unto our God. Many, seeing this, shall fear the Lord and put their trust in Him. Blessed is the man that setteth his hope on the Lord and turneth not unto the proud and unto such as go about with lies.' And did so proceed unto the end of the psalm, at the last verse whereof he rendered his spirit, as it had been without pain, to the great and most singular comfort of all faithful, and to the fear, confusion and shame of those cruel tyrants." [1]

[1] *Works*, iv. 301.

# CHAPTER III.

## THE SCOTTISH REFORMATION

MARY, QUEEN OF ENGLAND, having died on 17 November 1558 the exiles who were dispersed over the Continent, trooped home ; and in Geneva Knox had no longer a congregation to which to minister. Accordingly he left that city for good in the following January. But, for the reason already mentioned, he was not permitted to set foot in England, even for the purpose of passing through it to Scotland ; and it was not till the month of May that he arrived in Edinburgh. On his voyage, however, he became privy to a secret, which he hoped, not without reason, might yet open his way to the favour of Queen Elizabeth, which for the time he had forfeited. In the vessel in which he sailed there was a great seal, graven with the arms of France, England and Scotland, and with a style for the French king and queen, naming them king and queen of these three countries. Of this jewel, as he calls it, Knox procured a sight, and he treasured this as a state secret of importance, to be divulged at some favourable opportunity. The king and queen who thus made pretentions to the throne of England, in rivalry to Elizabeth, were the Dauphin, afterwards Francis II. of France, and Mary Stuart, afterwards the Queen of Scots, who had been wedded in 1558.

Knox's arrival in his native country took place at a critical moment; indeed, it proved to be so well-timed that devout students of history have recognised in this the special providence of God.

Three years had elapsed since his last visit; and in the interval the tide had been flowing strongly in favour of the Reformation. Mary of Lorraine, who had been Regent since 1554, had found it expedient in her own interest to encourage the Protestant nobles. These, in the year 1557, had formed an agreement among themselves, called the Band, in which they vowed to employ their whole power, substance and very lives to maintain, set forward and establish the blessed Word of God and of His congregation. From this time they were denominated the Lords of the Congregation, the Congregation being the name by which those who favoured the new religion were known. They were even so bold as to approach the Regent with a petition for the right of public and private prayer in the vulgar tongue, of explaining and expounding the Scriptures, and of communion in both kinds ; and they humbly required that means should be taken for the reform of the wicked, slanderous and detestable lives of prelates and the state ecclesiastical. In 1559 another Council met, which passed many resolutions for reform, the very terms of which are the best evidence of the charges made by Protestants against the old Church ; these measures, however, proved, like others which had preceded them, to be only reforms on paper, the Church being too corrupt to reform itself. Meanwhile the preachers of the Gospel were so multiplying in numbers and growing so bold that more than once the Regent summoned them to her presence, with the intention of silencing them ; but, when they appeared, they were accompanied by so many supporters that she was fain to dismiss them with nothing done.

At heart, however, she was a thorough papist, her secret determination being to subject the country religiously to the see of Rome and politically to the power of France. She had filled the country with French soldiers, who devoured it unmercifully and perpetrated every insolence ; and at length, after the crown matrimonial had been bestowed on her son-in-law, she considered that the hour had come for throwing off the mask. Accordingly the preachers were summoned to appear before her at Stirling on 10 May 1559. They prepared to obey the summons; but the men of Montrose and Dundee, with others from the surrounding parts of Forfarshire and Fife, accompanied them in arms as far as Perth; and in the Dundee contingent John Knox made his appearance, having arrived in Edinburgh on the second of the month.

The Regent had, in fact, evoked civil war, which went on without intermission till her death. Its first centre was Perth, between which place and Stirling, where the Queen Regent lay, complex negotiations went on. Meantime Knox was preaching in the Fair City, his voice rising like a trumpet over the confusion of the times; and in connection with his preaching there broke out the spoliation of the holy places of the old religion, which has been so often made a serious charge against him. According to his own account, this began accidentally. After a sermon against idolatry, a priest commenced to say Mass; whereupon a boy used some abusive language; whereat the priest struck him a blow; then the lad threw a stone, which struck the altar at which the priest was ministering; whereupon confusion broke loose, and none could stop it. Thus were the houses of the Grey and the Black Friars and the Charterhouse Monks destroyed " by the hands," says Knox, " not of the gentlemen, neither of them that were earnest professors, but of the rascal multitude." He and others, a little later, attempted to stop similar proceedings at the Abbey and the Palace of Scone, refusing to speak to the rioters from Dundee who had done the violence. But similar acts of desecration accompanied his preaching soon afterwards at St. Andrews; and the destructive mania spread far and wide to other places. Knox would have preferred an orderly destruction of the symbols of idolatry by the action of lawful authority; but it would, it is to be feared, be too much to say that, in case of its not being done in this way, he would have preferred that it should not be done at all. The saying, often attributed to him, that the nests must be pulled down if the rooks are to be got rid of, cannot be traced to any document emanating from him; but it has internal verisimilitude. His æsthetic sense was imperfectly developed. He probably saw that the buildings and their ornaments were well adapted for the worship which it was his business to abolish; and, if buildings better adapted to Protestant worship and yet conforming to the laws of good taste were not substituted for these, this may be less his fault than that of the careless generations of Protestants that have succeeded him.

The war shifted from Perth to Fife, where the insurgents gained a decisive advantage at Cupar Muir ; and, thereafter, they drove the Regent and her troops out of Stirling and Edinburgh to Haddington, where they rallied. Then the tide of fortune turned ; and the Congregation were severely beaten at Leith and driven, in a sorely shattered condition, to Stirling.

It was a strange war ; for the combatants were less the Scots themselves than the French on the one side and the English on the other ; and the issue seemed to depend on the number of auxiliaries the one foreign power or the other could be induced to furnish. Knox had an extraordinary part to play in it ; because he was not only the army chaplain, whose voice, as Randolph, the English ambassador, said, was able to put more life into men than five hundred trumpets continually bluster-ing in their ears, but he was, besides, the secretary of the Congregation, issuing manifestoes and penning despatches ; and he was negotiator and almost spy, going on a secret mission to England and haggling with the English Government about the sums of money they were to pay to the various Scottish nobles for their services. It was all necessary, he believed, in the sacred cause, and with his whole heart and mind he approved of the English alliance, while he was certainly politically right in seeking to deliver his country from the presence of the French, who were intolerable oppressors of the people ; but we are almost glad that Knox did not shine in such negotiations. He was perfectly well known to the enemy at Berwick, when he thought he was going about incognito ; once, when he suggested that the English soldiers who lent their swords to Scotland should make an equivocal explanation of their conduct, he was sharply rebuked by the English agent with whom he was dealing ; and once, when he had secured a large sum of money from the English Government, it was surprised and seized by the enemy on its way North. He was himself weary of this business before he had had it long in charge ; and it was well when it was taken out of his hands by young Lethington. But he endured incredible labours and sufferings in those eventful months. Often he was sick in body and sicker still in spirit. Yet he was the life and soul of the whole movement ; and in moments of despair, which happened not rarely, he was able to pour energy into the veins of his comrades and inspire them with fresh faith in God and in their enterprise.

What might have been the issue of the struggle, had it been prolonged, it is impossible to say; but, while it still hung in the balance, Mary of Lorraine died on 10 June 1660; and, immediately thereafter, by the Treaty of Edinburgh, it was settled that Francis and Mary should give up using the arms of England; that the French troops should depart from Scotland and no office of importance be held any more by a Frenchman; and that a parliament should be forthwith assembled, the acts of which should be as valid as if it had been summoned by the King and Queen. Thus the Congregation triumphed all along the line; and the way was clear for realising all the hopes with which Knox had returned to his native country.

On 1 August 1560 began the sittings of the most important parliament that ever met in Scotland. It was numerously attended; the presence of many of the barons or lairds being especially noteworthy—an estate of the realm which had long had the right of sitting in parliament but had made little or no use of the privilege till now, when it was stirred with religious impulses and perceived how political power might be wielded as a weapon in the war of righteousness. " I never," reported Randolph, the English ambassador, to his master,

" heard matters of so great import neither sooner dispatched nor with better will agreed to." Religion had the first place ; and a committee of ministers, of whom Knox was one, were called on to draw up a confession of faith, as a basis for all that was to follow. In four days the First Scottish Confession was put together ; and it was adopted by parliament article by article ; the opposite party having nothing to say for themselves beyond a feeble dissent from a very few. It was resolved that the spiritual estate, on account of false doctrine and dishonoured sacraments, should be henceforth excluded from voting in parliament. All doctrines and practices contrary to the new creed were condemned. The jurisdiction of the Pope within the realm was abolished. Finally, the celebration of the Mass was forbidden under penalty of confiscation for the first offence, banishment for the second, and death for the third.

Thus, at one swoop, was the structure, which it had taken hundreds of years to rear, brought to the ground ; and, although to the end of his life Knox was kept in constant anxiety as to the possible raising up again of what he would have called the spiritual Babylon, the work was never undone. This was the end of the papacy in Scotland ; and with it an era of darkness, superstition and spiritual tyranny passed away. Whatever might be the shape which the New Scotland might assume, at all events the misshapen fabric of Papal Scotland had perished of its own corruption and gone down, unhonoured and unwept, into the abyss of oblivion. Never was there a system which was more utterly unable to offer for itself any rational defence. When the bishops, who were present in parliament, held their peace, the Earl Marischal uttered a word worthy of repetition. ("It is long," remarked he, "since I have had some favour unto the truth and since that I have had a suspicion of the papistical religion ; but, I praise my God, this day has fully resolved me in the one and the other. For, seeing that my Lord Bishops, who for their learning can, and for the zeal that they bear to the verity would, as I suppose, gainsay anything that directly repugns to the verity of God ; seeing, I say, that the Lord Bishops here present speak nothing to the contrary of the doctrine proponed, I cannot but hold it to be the very truth of God, and the contrary to be deceivable doctrine. And, therefore, as far as in me lieth, I approve the one and damn the other. And yet more, I must vote, by way of protestation, that, if any persons ecclesiastical shall after this oppose themselves to this our Confession, they have no place nor credit, considering that they, having had long advisement and full knowledge of this our Confession, none is now found, in lawful, free and quiet assembly, to oppose themselves to that which we profess." [1]

But much still required to be done to provide a substitute for the system which had been abolished and to supply to Scotland what Knox was fond of calling "the face of a Church." Ministers of the right stamp were scarce ; and much care had to be taken in distributing them to the best advantage over the country. Knox was appointed to Edinburgh, or rather reappointed ; for he had been appointed the year before amidst the troubles of the civil war, and it was still felt that he was the man for this centre. Adam Heriot was sent to Aberdeen, William Christison to Dundee, John Row to Perth, Christopher Goodman to St. Andrews ; and so on. Five ministers of distinguished ability were appointed Superintendents, to be over extensive districts, in which they were "to plant and erect churches, to set order and appoint ministers ; " and these were John Spottiswood for Lothian, John Wynram for Fife, John Willock for Glasgow, Erskine of Dun for Angus and Mearns, John Carswell for Argyll and the Isles. For the support

[1] *History*, ii. 122.

of these and their successors provision had to be made ; but, for this and for the preparation of a comprehensive scheme for the government of the new Church, there was not time in the Parliament of 1560 ; and so to the same committee which had drawn up the Confession of Faith it was remitted to draw up a Book of Discipline, embodying all these things in preparation for a Parliament to be held the following year. Accordingly, at this task Knox and his comrades laboured with assiduity and soon had their report ready. But it met with unexpected opposition and was refused the sanction of Parliament, its outline being too ambitious for that generation, whose leaders characterized its proposals as " devout imaginations." Its purpose was to employ the property of the old Church for the support of the new, and for the equipment of a national scheme of education and poor relief ; but this was wrecked upon the compensation which it was supposed necessary to give to the actual holders of the property, many of whom were members of the nobility or related to the noble families of the land, on which their support would have fallen, had they been dispossessed.

But there was a motive behind of a still more serious kind. The example set in England of the spolia-tion of the monasteries had not been lost on Scotland ;

and there was a keen thirst, especially in the upper classes, for the property, which was acknowledged to be in excess of the needs of the preachers. The longer a settlement was delayed, the easier would it be for the landed proprietors to absorb into their own estates the possessions of the Church, as the incumbents, one by one, slipped away. By the avarice of the Scottish nobility the patriotic plans of Knox were to a large extent frustrated; and by the struggle with these landgrabbers, many of whom were professors of the Reformed religion, the rest of his life was embittered. The preachers were starved, some of them, it is alleged, actually dying of cold and hunger; young men were discouraged from entering the ministry; and the whole fabric of the new Church was stunted. It was well that an ecclesiastical body was called into existence as a counterpoise to Parliament, the first General Assembly being held in December 1560, and consisting of six ministers and forty-two elders. Many attempts were made to wreck this institution in its early years, one of these evoking from Knox the famous saying : " Take from us the freedom of Assemblies and take from us the Evangel " ; but the General Assembly was destined to outlive the Scottish Parliament itself and nearly every other national institution then in existence.

Whilst, however, these sweeping changes were taking place, there was one power with which the revolutionists were not sufficiently reckoning. This was the sovereign of the country. Mary Stuart, the only child of James V. and Mary of Guise, was born in sorrow, as her father was dropping into his grave a broken-hearted man. But she grew up gay and beautiful, with all the cleverness of the Stuart race in her brain and all its waywardness and passion in her blood. Scarcely had she come into the world when there was talk of marrying her ; and about this there was far too much talk, for her comfort, all her days. First, she was to be the bride of the son of the King of England ; and self-willed Harry the Eighth ravaged Scotland with fire and sword because this agreement was departed from, destroying, as he did so, not a few of those beautiful houses of religion on the Borders, the destruction of which is often credited to John Knox. Mary of Guise brought it about that her child was espoused to the Dauphin of her own native land ; and in 1548, at the age of six, the little maid was accordingly carried to France, to be educated for her great destiny under the eye of her future mother-in-law, the renowned Catherine de' Medici. It was an evil school ; for the French court was unspeakably corrupt. "She was sold," says Knox.

" to go to France, to the end that in her youth
she should drink of that liquor that should remain
with her all her lifetime, for a plague to this realm
and for her final destruction." [1] In 1558 she was
married, at the age of sixteen, to a husband six
weeks her junior, and she signed a secret deed,
making over her country and crown, in the event of
her death, to France, this compact to hold good
notwithstanding any declaration to the contrary
she might make in public, a fact which proves how
exactly she had been taught in the same school of
political morality as her mother, who declared at a
critical moment in her own life that princes ought
not to be bound by their promises any longer than
was compatible with their own convenience. The
Dauphin, Mary's husband, succeeded to the French
throne.the year after their marriage ; he was, however, but a sickly boy entirely under the thumb of
his ambitious mother ; and he died the following
year, in November 1560. Thus was taken away
one large portion of the glory apparently destined
for Mary, who at one time seemed likely to be Queen
at once of France, England and Scotland. It will be
remembered that her mother had died the same year ;
and now, after the double bereavement, the time
seemed ripe for her to return to her native country.

[1] *History*, i. 218.

On 19 August, 1561 ,accompanied by her four
Maries and a brilliant retinue, she landed at Leith ;
but it was one of those dismal days of rain, mist
and darkness for which the Scottish climate is
unrivalled ; and prophets after the event said that
it was a presage of all the misery which was
coming to the country and to her. The climate,
political and religious, into which she had come,
was scarcely less dismal for one born and bred
as she had been ; and, without treachery to the
cause of Knox, it is surely possible to extend
to the illfated princess a tribute of sympathy.
Hardly had she set foot on the soil of her country
when she became involved in the religious quarrel ;
for, the Sunday after her arrival, Mass was said
in the chapel of Holyrood. This acted on the
community like a spark on gunpowder, and the
flames of religious excitement enveloped the land.
Some stuck by the fact that she had broken the law
and incurred its penalty. Others said that she
could not avoid what had been done, having so
many French visitors at the palace. A rumour
spread that, if she were interfered with, she would
take ship and sail back to the place whence she
had come. Sanguine Protestants said that, if
she were treated with generosity, she might be won
to their side. Knox, from his pulpit in St. Giles',

declared that one Mass inspired him with more terror than would the landing in the country of ten thousand men.

Hearing of this sermon, Mary sent for the preacher to the palace, and interviewed him in the presence of the future Regent Moray. She reproached him with his book on female government ; but he skilfully parried this attack by declaring that it had always been the privilege of the learned to emit theories of government differing widely from the customs of their own day, as Plato had done in his *Republic* ; but yet they had lived quietly under the constitutions of their time and country. She then drew out of him his political views, the upshot of which appeared, she said, to be that her subjects were to obey him instead of her. But out of this conclusion also he extricated himself by the observation that the whole end of his preaching was to lead subjects and princes both to obey God. From this she drifted into the true papist's question, how she was to know whether he or the teachers of her youth had the divine authority ; to which his reply was that she was to trust neither the one nor the other, but God speaking in his Word. He left her with the benediction : " I pray God, Madam, that you may be as blessed within the commonwealth of Scotland, if it be the pleasure of God, as ever

Deborah was in the commonwealth of Israel."
What she thought of her visitor we have not been
informed ; but his opinion of her was, " If there be
not in her a proud mind, a crafty wit, and an in-
durate heart against God and His truth, my judgment faileth me."

It is difficult to know what attraction there was
in Knox which made Mary wish to see him any
more ; but she did send for him again and again ;
and it is evident from his accounts of these interviews that the attraction was not all on one side.
Mary appears to have hoped to subdue this son of
thunder.   He, perhaps, did not hope enough to subdue her ; for he seems early to have spoken strongly
of the hopelessness of her conversion.   But he
enjoyed the encounter of wits with so keen a mind.
It was not an entirely unequal contest ; for, while
he had the advantage of age and experience, she
had the advantage of being a woman and a
queen.

The second occasion of his being summoned to
the monarch's presence was a sermon he had preached
against an outbreak of persecution in France, where
the Huguenots had been attacked by the Guises, in
celebration of which the Queen was supposed to
have held a ball at Holyrood.   This time the
preacher was in a humorous mood, and hinted to

Mary that the ordinary fate of people who do not go to Church had befallen her, in that she had heard ill of herself, and did not know whether or not it was true. If she would come to the sermon, she would not be misinformed as she had been. Or, if she appointed time and place, he would come and preach his sermon over again to her. So he departed " with a reasonable merry countenance ; whereat some papists offended, said : ' He is not afraid.' Which heard of him, he answered, ' Why should the pleasing face of a gentlewoman make me afraid ? I have looked in the faces of many angry men, and yet have not been afraid above measure.' " [1]

It was Mary who was in a pleasant humour at their next interview, which took place at Lochleven, where she had invited him to attend her. The occasion was one of national interest. The Queen's example, as a papist and hearer of Mass, was rapidly telling on the country. People of high degree came up from the provinces hot against the ceremony which the law of the land condemned, but the atmosphere of the court cooled them, and they went home thinking the Mass was not so dangerous after all. Wherever Mary made her progresses, of which she was fond, as they were

[1] *History*, i. 335.

very popular, the Mass went with her; and the
nobility with whom she had been staying were
tempted to continue it after she had left. Knox's
best friends, like the future Regent Moray, had
dissented from his views, maintaining that the Queen
had the right to the exercise of her own religion;
and Calvin had even been appealed to against his
disciple. Many, of whom Lethington was one, had
gone completely over to the Queen's side, and were
her uncompromising apologists. At length the priests
of the old Church beginning to bestir themselves,
the Mass was celebrated here and there. But the
gentlemen of the West, ever the most resolute and
jealous Protestants in the country, taking the law
into their own hands, suppressed the unlawful
practice by force. Of this Knox approved, and
Mary summoned him to answer for it. They had
an angry interview in the evening; but next
morning, as she went out to the hawking, she
summoned him to her side and entered into the
most confidential conversation on matters concerning both his and her welfare; no allusion being
made to the subject of the preceding evening's discussion, till, at the moment of parting, she whispered
that all should be done as he had desired:
to which he replied: "I am assured then that
you shall please God and enjoy rest and tran-

quillity within your realm ; which to your Majesty
is more profitable than all the Pope's power can
be." [1]

Very different was the next interview, which
took place in June 1563, when it was rumoured
that the Queen was about to marry the son of the
King of Spain, of course a Catholic. On this
report Knox had commented in the pulpit with
such energy as to displease his own friends, and
flatterers were not slow to carry his words to the
court. On his arrival there he found the Queen in
a towering passion, which lasted throughout the entire
interview ; every attempt of his to explain himself
being met with the question : " But what have you to
do with my marriage " ? " I have borne with you,"
she exclaimed through her tears, " in all your
rigorous manner of speaking ; yea, I have sought
your favours by all possible means, and yet I cannot
be quit of you. I vow to God, I shall be revenged."
He pleaded that he was not his own master in the
pulpit, but had to utter what was given him. But
the same angry rejoinder burst from her ; and she
added the contemptuous question : " And what are
you within this realm ? " But it was now his turn
to score ; and he replied : " A subject born within
the same ; and, albeit I be neither earl, lord

[1] *History*, i. 376.

nor baron, yet has God made me, how abject I
ever be in your eyes, a profitable member thereof."
Erskine of Dun, who stood by, attempted to soothe
the enraged princess, but her tears and sobs re-
doubled ; and Knox was dismissed with an injunction
to wait in the ante-chamber till the royal pleasure
should be announced to him.   There he was avoided
by the courtiers, as if he had been a leper ; but
he turned him to the ladies of the court and said,
not in the tones of a terrified man : " O fair ladies,
how pleasant were this life of yours, if it should
ever abide, and then in the end you might pass
to heaven with all this gear.   But fye upon that
knave Death, that will come whether we will or
not."    And so on he moralised, availing himself of
the best company to be had in the circumstances,
till the storm in the inner chamber was allayed and
he was permitted to depart.[1]

From this time onwards, there can be no doubt
that Knox was in deadly peril ; and it was not
long before Mary thought she had caught him
in a corner from which escape was impossible.
In her absence from the city, Mass was said at
Holyrood in a peculiarly offensive manner during
the celebration of the Lord's Supper in the churches
of the town ; whereat Knox's party sent certain

[1] *History*, i. 389.

of their number to take note of the persons who
attended the service in the chapel. Out of this
sprang some disorder, which was greatly magnified ;
and two of the citizens of Edinburgh were arrested.
When they were about to be brought to trial,
Knox took it upon him to convene a number
of friends from different parts of the country,
to stand by the prisoners. His letter falling into
the hands of Mary, who regarded it as treason-
able, Knox was called to answer for this crime
before the Privy Council in December 1563. His
best friends counselled him to make his submission
to the Queen beforehand, as they could perceive
no way of escape. But Knox disdained to use
any artifice, saying : "I praise my God, through
Jesus Christ, I have learned not to cry conjuration
and treason at everything that the godless multitude
does condemn, neither yet to fear the things that
they fear.". The Queen came in and occupied
the chair with no little worldly pomp ; " But," adds
Knox, " her pomp lacked one principal point, to
wit, womanly gravity ; for, when she saw John
Knox standing at the other end of the table, bare-
headed, she first smiled, and then burst into laugh-
ter, saying : "Know ye whereat I laugh ? Yon
man made me weep,[1] and wept never a tear himself.

[1] " gart me greit."

I will see whether I can make him cry." The
Queen entered into the argument, and Secretary
Lethington did his very best to fasten the halter
round the neck of the culprit. But never was Knox
more cool and astute. They were assuming that
to convene the Queen's lieges without her permission
was manifestly a crime ; but Knox boldly denied
it, arguing that he did so every Sabbath, when
he invited people to Church ; he proved that he had
commission from the General Assembly to call
the friends of the Church together whenever public
necessity required it ; and there were those in
the Council who had answered such summonses
from his pen in days gone by. A stupor of
admiration seized the Council, like that which fell
on the tribunal of the beasts when Reineke Fuchs
made his defence, and they unanimously acquitted
the prisoner. So incensed was Lethington that
he recalled the Queen, who had left the chamber,
and caused the vote to be taken over again in
her presence. But Scottish nobles were not to
be thus intimidated ; and they gave the same votes
over again with the emphasis of indignation.[1] There
is not in history a scene more creditable to the
Scottish nobility ; but it robbed John Knox of
the martyr's crown.

[1] *History*, i. 412.

Still he might well have felt like David, when he said : " I shall one day fall into the hands of Saul." Mary's blandishments were slowly undermining the virtue of the Protestant nobility ; behind whom there was a considerable body of nobles still Catholic ; and, by serious riots in Edinburgh, it was made manifest that the common man resented the yoke of discipline imposed by the new system. Mary and Knox stood out more and more clearly as rival champions ; and an indifferent spectator of the struggle might have predicted with considerable confidence that the beautiful Queen would win in the long run. But by a sudden and overmastering impulse Mary flung her chances away, and the game was left in the hands of her grim antagonist.

There is nothing in the annals of romance more dramatic than the history of Mary, Queen of Scots, from her marriage to Darnley till her flight into England, from which she was never to return. The dates are eloquent, and ought to be carefully noted ; because they reveal the headlong haste with which the various stages of this veritable Prodigal's Progress were evolved.

After innumerable schemes for her second marriage had been discussed, Mary made a choice of her own, wedding her cousin, Henry Darnley, on 29 July

1565, she being then twenty-three and he nineteen
years of age. This step cost her the loss of her
best counsellors, such as the future Regent Moray
and Maitland of Lethington, and made Queen
Elizabeth and the statesmen of England her enemies.
But her cousin had a handsome person and a fair
face, and without regard for consequences she obeyed
the impulse of her heart. Love, however, which
swelled like the Solway, ebbed like its tide. Darnley
was a fool, and she was soon disgusted with him,
making no more secret of her dislike than she had
previously done of her favour. On Rizzio, an
Italian, who had come to Scotland in the train of
the ambassador of Savoy and stayed as a secret
agent of the Pope, she allowed her affections to
decline, and she loaded him with promotions, which
rendered him so obnoxious to the Scottish nobility
that several of its members, in conjunction with
the jealous Darnley, stabbed him to death in the
Queen's ante-chamber on 9 March, 1566. Such an
act was not likely to bring back to her husband
Mary's wandering affections : and now she fell under
the spell of another and still more dangerous
lover, James Hepburn, Earl of Bothwell, whom
Throgmorton, a keen observer, had, years before,
described to Queen Elizabeth as "a glorious, rash
and hazardous young man." At the baptism of

her son, the future James VI., in the June of this
year, Bothwell was allowed to take a prominent
part, while Darnley, the father of the child, was
banished from the ceremony. In October Mary
paid Bothwell a romantic visit at Hermitage Castle
on the Border, riding so far and so fast for the
purpose as to bring on a dangerous illness. On
9 February of the following year Darnley was
foully murdered by an explosion of gunpowder at
Kirk-o'-Field, a spot on which the University of
Edinburgh now stands but then outside the city ;
and Bothwell was universally believed to be the
leader of the conspirators, although he was acquitted
at a mock trial. Three months afterwards, on
15 May 1567, Mary married him, after creating
him Duke of Orkney ; he having in the beginning
of the month, through the shameful connivance
of the head of the Roman Catholic Church,
obtained a divorce from his wife. Mary was
ready to launch forth on a new career, youth
at the prow and pleasure at the helm ; but she
had miscalculated the temper of a Protestant
population. By a common impulse the country
rose up in an access of disgust and horror. The
troops which she summoned to her assistance
melted away on Carberry Hill. She was separated
forever from her paramour and brought a prisoner

to the capital, amidst the most humiliating out-
breaks of popular execration.  She had to sign her
own demission of the crown ; her infant son was
crowned king ; Moray was appointed regent of
the kingdom ; and she was imprisoned in Lochleven
Castle.   Thence she managed to make her escape
in May 1568 ; but, although three-fourths of the
nobility flocked to her standard, she was so de-
cisively beaten in a single battle at Langside that
she had to flee to England, where, for nearly twenty
years, she remained in confinement, till in 1587, in
Fotheringay Castle, she laid her head on the
block and terminated her tragic career.

During all these proceedings Knox took the worst
possible view of Mary, not scrupling to apply to
her terms unfit for ears polite ; and in his opinion
a grave iniquity was committed when she was
not tried and executed for murder and adultery,
instead of being imprisoned in Lochleven Castle ;
for, in his eyes, birth or rank was no excuse for
crime.   But, as by the death of Mary of Lorraine
his cause was saved from impending danger, so by
the frailties of Mary Stuart it secured its second
great deliverance and victory, at a juncture when it
appeared to be in imminent peril.   Knox preached
at the coronation of the infant King at Stirling and
again at the opening of Parliament at the close

of the year. The Regent Moray, from whom he had long been alienated on account of their differing views as to the extent to which the Queen should be tolerated in the exercise of her own religion, was now his intimate friend again ; and they laboured with one mind and heart for the best interests of the kingdom. As early as December 1567, the General Assembly could write to John Willock, whom it was recalling from England, that he might help in forwarding the good work in Scotland : " Our enemies, praised be God, are dashed ; religion established ; sufficient provision made for ministers ; orders taken, and penalty appointed for all sort of transgressions and transgressors ; and, above all, a godly magistrate, whom God, of His eternal and heavenly providence, hath reserved to this age, to put in execution whatever He by His law commandeth."

# CHAPTER IV.

## CLOSING YEARS

ON the accession of Moray to the regentship,
Knox was sent by the Assembly to visit
the congregations between Stirling and Berwick to
foster in the population a spirit favourable to the
new government. And this was not the first
occasion on which he had been absent for a considerable time from his own pulpit, impressing his
personality on the country at large. More than
once during Mary's reign he had been silenced in
Edinburgh or banished from the city; and these
opportunities were utilised for far-extended visitations
in different parts of the country. Once he even
went into England; but this was for the purpose of
seeing his two sons, who were being brought up by
the relatives of their mother. But the Church of St.
Giles was still his watchtower, from which he took a
keen and wide survey of the political and religious
horizon; and the numbers of his devoted disciples
grew ever greater in the capital. They looked

carefully after his temporal interests and, when the court endeavoured to silence or banish him, they made vigorous protest. Even from distant parts of Scotland, when his life was in peril, warnings came to the authorities from bodies of men, who made it manifest that they were not to be trifled with.

The Good Regent, however, as Moray came to be called, had many enemies, and he was well aware that he was carrying his life in his hand. At length he was assassinated at Linlithgow on 23 January 1570.[1] This was the most shattering trial of Knox's life; and, although at the funeral he preached so as to move three thousand persons to shed tears for the loss of such a good and godly governor, he felt that his share in the affairs of this world was drawing to an end ; and, before the close of the year, he experienced a shock of apoplexy.

Queen Mary still had a strong party in the country, who desired her return to the throne ; and of course the removal of the Good Regent encouraged their designs. Among them the most prominent were Maitland of Lethington and Kirk-caldy of Grange—the one the ablest lawyer and the other the strongest soldier of the age. Both had at one time been disciples of Knox ; but now the old man looked on them as backsliders and

[1] SIR THOMAS GRAINGER-STEWART: *The Good Regent.*

denounced them in very plain terms from the pulpit
Both, at different times, took the constitutional
course of complaining of these attacks to the Kirk
Session ; Kirkcaldy's letter of complaint being one
of great spirit and earnestness.[1]   But they were not
likely to gain more by this means than did the
French Ambassador, who, on one occasion, having
complained to the Town Council of the freedom
with which Knox had, in the pulpit, handled the
name of his royal master, was informed by that
body that, so far from being able to assist him,
they were not always able to prevent John Knox
from denouncing themselves !   Kirkcaldy, however,
held Edinburgh Castle ; and he managed to make
the city so hot for Knox, through whose window
a shot was fired one night, the ball lodging in
the part of the wall in front of which he usually
sat, that the friends of the preacher persuaded
him, though with great difficulty, to remove for
a time to St. Andrews.

Kirkcaldy's attacks were, however, coarse in comparison with the skilful thrusts of Lethington, which,
for many years, were a source of constant irritation
and pain to theReformer ; who, however, in dealing
with them, revealed the gladiatorial skill of which
he was capable, even in old age.   Thus, in March 1571,

[1] *Works*, vi. 577.

in answer to an anonymous libel, with which it
is too probable Lethington was connected, Knox
replies: " I am not a man of the law, to have my
tongue to sell for silver or favour of the world."
" Railing and sedition," he remarks, " they are never
able to prove in me, till that first they compel Isaiah,
Jeremiah and Ezekiel, St. Paul, and others to recant ;
of whom I have learned plainly and boldly to call
wickedness by its own name, a fig a fig, and a
spade a spade." And he winds up with this
memorable outburst: " What I have been to my
country, albeit this unthankful age will not know,
yet the ages to come will be compelled to bear
witness to the truth. And thus I cease, requiring
of all men who have anything to object against me
that they will do it as plainly as that I make
myself and all my doings manifest to the world ;
for to me it seems a thing most unreasonable that,
in this my decrepit age, I should be compelled to
fight against shadows and howlats[1] that dare not
abide the light." [2]

Maitland probably treated with contempt the
solemn warnings hurled by the Reformer against
himself and Kirkcaldy. But less than a year had
elapsed after the last of these utterances before
the earthly career of both had been ignominiously

---

[1] owls.      [2] *Works*, vi. 596.

ended ; Lethington dying in prison, not without leaving behind the suspicion that he had released himself " the Roman way " from the complications in which he had become hopelessly entangled ; and Kirkcaldy perishing on the scaffold, after confessing that it would have been good for him if he had followed the counsel of John Knox, whose prophecies had been fulfilled.

Knox was an old man when he was driven from Edinburgh to sojourn in St. Andrews ; and of his venerable appearance at this time we have received from James Melville, then a student there, a description which is one of the gems of biography :—

"Of all the benefits that I had that year (1571) was the coming of that most notable Prophet and Apostle of our nation, Master John Knox, to St. Andrews. I heard him teach the Prophecy of Daniel. I had my pen and my little book, and took away such things as I could comprehend. In the opening up of his text he was moderate the space of half-an-hour. But, when he entered to application, he made me so to grue and tremble that I could not hold the pen to write. He would sometimes come in and repose himself in our College Yard. He would call us scholars unto him and bless us, and exhort us to know God and His work in our country, and to stand by the good

cause. I saw him every day of his doctrine go
hulie and fear, with a furring of martricks about
his neck, a staff in the one hand, and good, godly
Richard Bannatyne, his servant, holding up the
other oxter from the Abbey to the Parish Church.
Then, by the same Richard and another servant,
he was lifted up to the pulpit, where he behoved
to lean at his first entrance ; but, ere he had done
with his sermon, he was so active and vigorous that
he was like to ding the pulpit in blads [1] and fly
out of it." To all the inhabitants of the ancient
seat of learning, however, the presence of Knox was
not so acceptable ; he became involved there in more
than one of those disputes with which small university towns are incessantly agitated ; and his
experience made him leave to the Church, as a
solemn legacy, the advice : " Above all things preserve the Kirk from the bondage of the Universities."

It was here that he was brought into momentary
contact with a movement which was to have
enduring importance for the Church, but of which
even his penetration did not at the time foresee
the issues. The Government, under the regency of
the Earl of Mar, was pressed for money ; and again
the plan of squeezing it out of the Church was
resorted to. It was in the brain of the Earl of

[1] break in pieces.

Morton, subsequently Regent, that the device of Tulchan Bishops was fabricated—that is, of reviving the office of bishop, but only for the purpose of allowing the Government with a show of legality to draw the salary, while the incumbent contented himself with a small moiety of the same. One of these new prelates was appointed Archbishop of St. Andrews while Knox was there; but the aged Reformer refused to bear any part in the proceedings. He is said to have had no conscientious objections to the office itself; but, at all events, Beza, with whom he was corresponding on the subject, gave no uncertain warning of the danger which, in no long time, was to become manifest enough in Scotland.

In August 1572 Knox returned to Edinburgh; and, the same month, came from France the news of the Massacre of St. Bartholomew. Once more all the fire of his nature blazed up in a denunciation which he pronounced from the pulpit of St. Giles' against the latest act of that bloody House, which he looked upon as the worst enemy of Scotland and of Protestantism. But this was almost the last effort of his declining strength. They had to partition off a little space in his great church, where he could still preach to a few, when his voice was too weak to overtake the multitude. He had the felicity of seeing a colleague—James Lawson from Aberdeen—settled over his old congregation; and his own very last appearance in public was at the induction of Lawson on 9 November.

At length he who had encountered so many adversaries was called upon to meet the last enemy; and it was given him to do so not only so as to enjoy comfort himself but to leave also to his friends and to posterity the assurance that he had obtained the victory.[1] Two days after the induction of Lawson, he was taken with a sore cough, which annoyed and enfeebled him. Paying his servant, Jamie Campbell, his wages that day, he added: "Thou wilt get no more of me in this life"; and so he gave him twenty shillings extra. On Friday he rose about his accustomed hour, but was unable to stand; and, when asked for what purpose he rose, he said that he was going to Church to preach, for he thought it had been Sunday; all night he had been meditating on the resurrection of Christ, on which he was to discourse after doing so on His death; many times he had prayed that he might end his ministry by preaching on that doctrine. On Saturday he was able to sit down at table for

[1] Narratives by Bannatyne and Lawson in *Works*, vi.

the last time ; two acquaintances, John Durie and Archibald Stewart, dining with him. He caused pierce a hogshead of wine which was in the cellar, "and willed the said Archibald to send for the same as long as it lasted ; for he would not tarry till it was drunken." On Sunday he kept his bed but desired the office-bearers of the Church to come and see him. This they did next day ; and he was able to speak, reviewing his ministry among them and exhorting them so tenderly that they departed with tears. But, retaining Lawson and Lindsay, he directed them to carry a last message of warning to Kirkcaldy of Grange in the Castle ; "For," said he, "the man's soul is dear unto me, and I would not have it perish, if I could save it." He was the worse of the effort to address the representatives of the congregation and could not afterwards speak without pain. Still he had an apt word for everyone who came to visit him ; and many did so, among them Lord Boyd, Lord Morton, Lord Lindsay, Lord Ruthven and Lord Glencairn.

When a pious gentlewoman began to praise God for what he had been, he turned on her with, "Tongue ! tongue ! lady ; flesh of itself is over-proud and needs no means to esteem itself." On another occasion, coming out of a fit of abstraction, in which he had exhibited signs of deep distress, he said : " I have before this sustained many conflicts in this frail life and many assaults from Satan, but at this time that roaring lion hath most furiously attacked me and put forth all his strength, that he might devour and make an end of me at once. Often before hath he placed my sins before my eyes, often tempted me to despair, often has he endeavoured to entangle me with the allurements of the world ; but, these weapons being broken by the sword of the Spirit, which is the Word of God, he could accomplish nothing. But now he has attacked me in another way ; for the cunning serpent has endeavoured to persuade me that I have merited heaven itself and a blessed immortality by the faithful discharge of the ministerial office committed to me. But blessed be God, who suggested to me those passages of Scripture by which I was able to grapple with him and ex- tinguish this fiery dart ; among which were these, " What hast thou that thou hast not received ? 'and, " By the grace of God I am what I am ; " and, " Not I, but the grace of God in me " ; and, thus being vanquished, he went away ; wherefore I give thanks to my God by Jesus Christ, who was pleased to grant me the victory. I am firmly persuaded that he will not attack me further, but that, in a short time, without any great bodily pain and without any distress of mind, I shall exchange this mortal and miserable life for an immortal and blessed life, through Jesus Christ."

On Friday he gave orders to Richard Bannatyne, his secretary, to get his coffin made ready. One more Sunday he was spared, and, when most of the family were at Church, he lay thinking, till he burst out to a friend who had continued beside him: "These two last nights I have been in meditation on the Kirk of God, the Spouse of Jesus Christ, despised of the world but precious in His sight, I have called to God for her, and committed her to her Spouse, Jesus Christ. I have been fighting against Satan, who is ever ready to assault; yea, I have fought against spiritual wickedness in heavenly things and have prevailed. I have been in heaven and have possession, and I have tasted of the heavenly joys, where presently I am." After Church many came in to see him; and, when asked if he had any pain, he replied: "No more pain than he that is now in heaven. I am content, if God so please, to lie here for seven years."

Monday, 24 November, was his last day on earth. He rose and put on some of his clothes, but was persuaded to go to bed again in the forenoon. To an old friend, Robert Campbell of Kinzeancleugh, he said: "I must leave the care of

my wife and bairns unto you, to whom you must
be a husband in my room." Daily those around
his bed had been wont to read to him favourite
passages of Scripture, such as Isaiah liii. and the
Epistle to the Ephesians, together with portions
of the Psalter, and certain sermons of Calvin.
This last day, he caused his wife to read 1 Corin-
thians xv. and, when it was ended, exclaimed :
" Is not that a comfortable chapter ? " At five
o'clock he said to her again : " Go read where I
cast my first anchor," meaning John xvii. It was
late at night before the last struggle set in. Hearing
him give a long sigh and a sob, his servant Richard
sat down before the bed and said : " Now sir, the
time that you have long called to God for, to wit,
an end of your battle, is come. And, seeing all
natural power now fails, remember upon those
comfortable promises which oftentimes you have
shown us of our Saviour Jesus Christ. And, that we
may understand and know that you hear us, make
us some sign." And so he lifted up one hand and
immediately thereafter rendered his spirit, sleeping
away without pain about eleven at night.

" On this manner," as the faithful Richard remarks,
" departed this man of God, the light of Scotland,
the comfort of the Kirk within the same, the mirror
of godliness, and a pattern and example to all true

ministers in purity of life, soundness of doctrine, and boldness in reproof of wickedness." No better inscription could have been placed on his tombstone; but the sentence of the Regent Morton, uttered at the side of his open grave, is the epitaph which has caught the fancy of posterity and sums up the veneration and gratitude of his fellow-countrymen: " Here lies one who never feared the face of man."

# BOOK SECOND

## *HIS IDEA*S

# CHAPTER I.

## HIS BOOKS

IN the preface to the only sermon of his ever published Knox says : " Wonder not, Christian reader, that of all my study and travail within the Scriptures of God these twenty years I have set forth nothing in expounding any portion of Scripture except this only rude and indigested sermon, preached by me in the public audience of the Church of Edinburgh the day of the year above mentioned. That I did not, in writing, communicate my judgment upon the Scriptures, I have ever thought and yet think myself to have most just reason. For, considering myself rather called of my God to instruct the ignorant, comfort the sorrowful, encourage the weak, and rebuke the proud, by tongue and lively voice, in these most corrupt days, than to compose books for the age to come, seeing that so much is written, and that by men of most singular condition, and yet so little observed, I decreed to contain myself within the bounds of that vocation whereunto I found myself especially called." In spite, however, of this modest disclaimer, Knox is a fairly voluminous author ; his works, in the classical edition of David Laing, filling six considerable volumes. Many of them were, indeed, so occasional, called forth by the demands of the hour, that he may hardly have thought of them as serious efforts in literature ; but the character thus impressed upon them—of casts taken straight from events—lends to them for posterity a peculiar value ; and, together, they at the same time afford a tolerably sufficient image of the author's mind.

Let us run through the list of Knox's works, adding a few words of description and quoting a few brief passages especially characteristic of the mind by which they were produced.

1. *An Epistle to the Congregation of the Castle of St. Andrews, with a Brief Summary of Balnaves on Justification by Faith.* 1548, written on board the galley of *Nôtre Dame.* 24 pages.

"That ye may plainly know," he remarks in the preface, " whereby are Satan and the world overcome, and which are the weapons against which they may not stand, ye shall read diligently this

work following ; which, I am sure, no man having
the Spirit of God shall think tedious or long,
because it contains 'nothing except the very
Scriptures of God and meditations of His law ;
wherein is the whole study of the godly man both
day and night, knowing that therein are found only
wisdom, prudence, liberty and life. And, therefore,
in reading, talking or meditation thereof he is never
satiate. But, as for the ungodly, because their
works are wicked, they may not abide the light.
And therefore they abhor all godly writings, thinking
them tedious though they contain not the length of
the Lord's Prayer."

2. *A Vindication of the Doctrine that the Sacrifice
of the Mass is Idolatry.* 1550, delivered at Durham,
in the presence of Bishop Tonstall and other
principalities and powers. A highly characteristic
utterance, clothed in the form of a scholastic disputation. 37 pages.

3. *A Summary, according to the Holy Scriptures,
of the Sacrament of the Lord's Supper.* Same date.
A supplement to the preceding treatise, setting
forth what the Lord's Supper is, after it has been
proved what it is not. 3 pages.

4. *A Declaration of the True Nature of Prayer.*
1553, before Knox had quitted England, after the
death of King Edward VI., to whom a pathetic

reference is made in a prayer at the end for the new Queen. 20 pages.

5. *An Exposition upon the Sixth Psalm of David.* Addressed to Mrs. Bowes. 1554, written at Dieppe, when Knox was escaping from England. The hold which England had taken of his heart during the years he had been a preacher there is indicated in the following sentences : " My daily prayer is for the sore afflicted in those quarters. Sometimes I have thought that impossible it had been so to have removed my affection from the realm of Scotland that any realm or nation could have been equally dear unto me. But God I take to record in my conscience, that the troubles present and appearing to be in the realm of England are doubly more dolorous unto my heart than ever were the troubles of Scotland." 37 pages.

6. *A Godly Letter of Warning or Admonition to the Faithful in London, Newcastle and Berwick.* 1554, dated " upon my departure from Dieppe, whither God knoweth." This is an affectionate message to those among whom he had laboured in England, and contains many interesting references to his own life there. Its aim is to warn against the idolatry of the Mass, and it contains a sustained comparison between the condition of England and that of Judah in the days of Jeremiah. 51 pages.

3427.

7. *Certain Questions concerning Obedience to Lawful Magistrates, with Answers by Bullinger.* 1554. Extracted from the correspondence of Bullinger, the Reformer of Zurich, with whom Knox became acquainted during his wanderings abroad, after he had been exiled from England. 6 pages.

8. *Two Comfortable Epistles to his Afflicted Brethren in England.* 1554, written from Dieppe, to which he had returned in the hope of hearing news from across the Channel. " My own estate is this," says he in the first of these documents : " since the 28 January I have travelled through all the congregations of Helvetia, and have reasoned with all the pastors and many other excellently learned men upon such matters as now I cannot commit to writing ; gladly I would by tongue or by pen utter the same to God's glory." 18 pages.

9. *A Faithful Admonition to the Professors of God's Truth in England.* 1554, written from Dieppe, where Knox was still sojourning, in the hope of receiving news from the opposite side of the Channel. 67 pages.

This is one of his most slashing productions. One item of news that had been wafted across from England to Dieppe was the impending marriage of the Queen to Philip of Spain, the head of the Catholic party in Europe. To both husband and wife he refers in terms the reverse of parliamentary, saying of the latter that "under an English name she beareth a Spanish heart." But the following outbreak against Gardiner, the persecuting Bishop of Winchester, may be quoted as a classical example of what Knox was able to do in the way of invective :—

"And what is the cause that Winchester, and the rest of his pestilent sect, so greedily would have a Spaniard to reign over England? The cause is manifest. For, as that whole nation surmounteth all others in pride and whoredom, so for idolatry and vain papistical and devilish ceremonies they may rightly be called the very sons of superstition. And therefore are they found and judged by the progeny of Antichrist most apt instruments to maintain, establish and defend the kingdom of that cruel beast, whose head and wound is lately cured within England, which, alas for pity! must now be brought into bondage and thraldom, that pestilent papists may reign without punishment. But, O thou beast!—I speak to you, Winchester— more cruel than any tiger, shall neither shame, neither fear, neither benefits received bridle thy tyrannous cruelty? Art thou not ashamed, bloody beast, to betray thy native country and the liberties of the same? Fearest thou not to open such a door to all iniquity, that whole England shall be made a common stew to Spaniards? Wilt thou recompense the benefits which thou hast received of that noble realm with such ingratitude? Rememberest thou not that England hath brought thee forth? that England hath nourished thee? that England hath promoted thee to riches, honour and high promotion? And wilt thou now, O wretched caitiff! for all these manifold benefits received, be the cause that England shall not be England? Yea, verily, for so wilt thou gratify thy father the Devil and his lieutenant the Pope, whom with all his baggage thou labourest now, with tooth and nail, to flourish again in England. Albeit, like a dissembling hypocrite and double-faced wretch, thou, being thereto compelled by the invincible verity of God's holy Word, wrotest long ago thy book, entitled *True Obedience*, against that monstrous whore of Babylon and her falsely usurped power and authority, now to thy perpetual shame thou returnest to thy vomit, and art become an open arch-papist again. Furthermore, why seekest thou the blood of Thomas, Archbishop of Canterbury, of good Father Hugh Latimer, and of that most earnest and discreet man, Doctor Ridley, true Bishop of London? Dost thou not consider that the lenity, the sincere doctrine, pure life, godly conversation and discreet counsel of these three is notably known in more realms than England ? Shamest thou not to seek the destruction of those who laboured for the safeguard of thy life and obtained the same, when thou justly deservedst death ?　O thou son of Satan, well declarest thou that nothing can mollify the cruel malice nor purge the deadly venom of him in whose heart the Devil beareth dominion.　Thou art brother to Cain and fellow to Judas, the traitor ; and therefore canst thou do nothing but thirst the blood of Abel and betray Jesus Christ and His eternal verity." [1]

It was this tract that was employed for the purpose of chasing Knox from Frankfort, as has been mentioned above ; and his opponents on that occasion made the following extraordinary statement about the effects it produced in England : " This we can assure you, that that outrageous pamphlet of Knox's added much oil to the flame of perse-cution in England.　For, before the publication of that work, not one of our brethren had suffered death ; but, as soon as it came forth, we doubt not but that you are well aware of the number of excellent men who have perished in the flames ; to say nothing of how many other godly men besides have been exposed to the risk of all their

[1] *Works*, iii. 297-9.

property, and even life itself, upon the sole ground
of either having had this book in their possession
or having read it; who were perhaps rescued from
the sword at greater cost and danger of life than
the others offered their necks to it." But it is not
to be forgotten that this statement comes from
partisans, whose notions, as their own last words
appear to prove, were not as clear as their prejudices
were emphatic.

The whole treatise, it may be added, is in the
form of a commentary on the miracle of Christ
walking on the water; and its purpose is to warn
professing Christians against the sin of attending
Mass, "under pretence that they may keep faith
secretly in the heart and yet do as idolaters do,
begin now to fall before that idol."

10. *A Letter to the Queen Dowager, Regent of Scotland.* 1556, written during Knox's momentous visit to
Scotland on the occasion of his marriage. It was
republished in 1558, in an augmented but certainly
not improved version. In its original form it might
be quoted as a good example of Knox's style,
when he wrote under the restraint of good sense
and good feeling; but he marred it in the second
edition by giving way to angry passion. 10 pages.

11. *An Exposition upon Matthew iv., concerning
the Temptation of Christ in the Wilderness.* 1556,

delivered as a sermon in Scotland and written out subsequently at the request of some hearer. It is an unfinished production, these words beginning the last paragraph : " Sundry impediments now do call me from writing in this matter ; but, by God's grace, at convenient leisure, I purpose to finish and to send unto you. I grant, the matter that proceedeth from me is not worthy your labour and pains to read it ; yet, seeing it is a testimony of my good mind towards you, I doubt not but you will accept it in good part." 20 pages.

12. *Answers to some Questions concerning Baptism.* 1556, apparently also connected with the same visit to Scotland. The question is whether baptism in the Roman Church is valid, or whether Protestants require to be rebaptized. There are also questions about the eating of blood and about tithes. 10 pages.

13. *A Letter of Wholesome Counsel, addressed to his Brethren in Scotland.* 1556, as he was leaving the country. 8 pages.

14. *The Form of Prayers and Ministration of the Sacraments used in the English Congregation at Geneva.* 1556, Knox being then minister there. 57 pages.

15. *Letters to his Brethren and the Lords professing the Truth in Scotland.* 1557, written from Dieppe, on the occasion of a false start for Scotland. Refers to two new dangers to the cause—false teachers

and dissolute preachers even among Protestants. 26 pages.

16. *An Apology for the Protestants who are holden in Prison at Paris; translated from the French with Additions.* 1557, written at Dieppe, where Knox was waiting for news from Scotland. The Additions are in his liveliest manner. 49 pages.

17. *The First Blast of the Trumpet against the Monstrous Regiment of Women.* 1558. "Regiment" means Government. 60 pages.

18 *The Appellation from the Sentence pronounced by the Bishops and Clergy: addressed to the Nobility and Estates of Scotland.* 1558, written before his final return to Scotland. At the close of his previous visit, the Romanists had burnt him in effigy, after degrading him from the priesthood and consigning his soul to hell and his body to the tender mercies of the secular arm. Knox appeals first, as Luther had done, to a General Council, but also to the nobility of his native land, against the machinations of " false prophets, flattering friars, and other such venomous locusts." 53 pages.

19. *A Letter addressed to the Commonalty of Scotland.* 1558, same occasion. 15 pages.

20. *An Epistle to the Inhabitants of Newcastle and Berwick.* 1558, written from Geneva; seems to indicate that the persecutions of Mary Tudor had

nearly obliterated the work of the Reformation in the North of England. 19 pages.

21. *A Brief Exhortation to England, for the Speedy Embracing of the Gospel.* 1558, same occasion. Subjoined is a list of the names of the martyrs who had suffered during the reign of Bloody Mary. 20 pages.

22. *An Answer to the Cavillations of an Adversary respecting the Doctrine of Predestination.* 1560. 448 pages.

23. *The Reasoning betwixt the Abbot of Crossraguel and John Knox concerning the Mass.* 1562. This disputation took place at Maybole in September of this year, and the Abbot of Crossraguel was Quentin Kennedy, son of the Earl of Cassilis, born 1520, died 1564. He was the author of several works in defence of the old Church ; but on this occasion he behaved like a sulking salmon, which no skill of the angler can move ; for he dived to the bottom at the very commencement of the argument, alleging that the Mass was typified by the bread and wine offered by Melchizedec to Abraham ; and Knox endeavoured in vain to broaden the scope of the discussion. 48 pages.

24. *A Sermon on Isaiah xxvi.* 13-21, *preached in St. Giles' Church, Edinburgh,* 19 *August* 1565. For preaching this sermon, which gave offence to

Darnley, who heard it, Knox was silenced ; and he printed it in self-vindication.   44 pages.

25. *The Book of Common Order ; or the Form of Prayers and Ministration of the Sacraments approved and received by the Church of Scotland.*   1564.

26. *The Order of the General Fast and the Form of Excommunication approved by the General Assembly of the Church of Scotland.*   1566.   78 pages.

27. *An Answer to a Letter written by James Tyrie, a Scottish Jesuit.*   1572.   Tyrie had endeavoured to convert his own brother, a Protestant, to the old faith, " with all the dog eloquence that Satan can devise for suppressing the free progress of the Evangel of Jesus Christ " ; and the brother requested Knox to write an answer.   40 pages.

28. *Letters* by, to, and about Knox. These extend from 1553 to 1572. The majority of them are addressed to female correspondents and reveal a side of Knox's personality which Mr. Taylor Innes has delineated with inimitable sympathy and insight in a chapter of his *John Knox* entitled " His Women Friends."   230 pages.

29. *The History of the Reformation of Religion within the Realm of Scotland.* This is Knox's masterpiece, and forms vols. i. and ii. of his Collected Works. He was moved to undertake it by the Lords of the Congregation, who desired a

vindication of their conduct towards Mary of Lorraine
to be placed on record.    In fulfilment of this instruction he penned Books II. and III., which supply
an account by a keen eye-witness of the most
momentous years of Scottish history——that is to say,
from the commencement of the struggle with Mary
of Lorraine to the arrival of Mary Queen of Scots
in the country ; the author printing verbatim the
documents on both sides, in which the very soul
of the struggle was embodied.    He was afterwards
persuaded to add Book I., in order to explain the
historical origin of the Reformation, by going back
to the earliest efforts towards reform, and especially
to the fortunes of his own predecessors, Hamilton
and Wishart.    In 1556, when Queen Mary had
upset her own throne, Knox added Book IV., the
most interesting of all, in which occur his interviews
with the Queen ; the story being brought down to
1564.    Book V. is a compilation by an editor, who
made use of papers left by Knox in an unfinished
state ; it brings the story down to 1566.

As Dr. Hume Brown has well observed, the most
prominent characteristic of Knox as a historian is
his abounding vitality.    " From the ' meary bourds '
with which he enlivens his narrative we may infer
that his daily conversation was not always of
justification and predestination ; but that he could

tell his story and exchange his jest as time and place were fitting. What distinguishes him from men like Calvin or Savonarola is precisely that sense of a humorous side of things, which made him at once a great writer and a great leader of men. Of the value of this quality in the conduct of human affairs he was himself perfectly conscious, and deliberately employed it, both in his writings and in his dealings with his fellows. 'Melancholius ressouns,' he said in one of his debates with Lethington, 'wald haif sum myrth intermixed.' Studied anticlimax, grim irony, humorous exaggeration are as distinctively his characteristics as they are those of Carlyle, in whom also these are relieving qualities to narrow intensity and an overbearing temper. With humour is usually found pity and the power of pathos ; and in Knox, more than once, his harsh austerity softens into a mood the more impressive that it comes so seldom." [1] He has the power, which someone has ascribed to Dante, of seizing a character by the scalp, bending back the head, and imprinting on the brow an ineffaceable brand. The instinct for documents, the power of vision and the power of expression, with a patriotism which enables him to sympathize with the fortunes of the country the history of which he is narrating,

[1] HUME BROWN : *John Knox*, ii. 224.

may be mentioned among his prominent qualities as a historian. Of the last-mentioned quality a little trait occurs to me, in which Knox describes the treatment of " a born Scottish man," by one of the French soldiery imported by Mary of Lorraine : " There was a poor craftsman, who had bought for his victuals a grey loaf, and was cutting a morsel of it, and was putting the rest of it in his bosom. The tyrant came to him and, with the poor caitiff's own whinger, first struck him in the breast and, after, cast it at him ; and so, the poor man staggering and falling, the merciless tyrant ran him through with his rapier, and thereafter commanded him to be hanged over the stair. Lord, Thou wilt yet look, and recompense such tyranny, how contemptible that ever the person was."

One or two specimens may be given of the author's most characteristic vein ; and in the second of these it will be noticed that he is dealing with a subject—the martyrdom of Wishart—in which, it is certain, his deepest feelings were engaged ; and yet he cannot refrain from giving way to a derisive and sarcastic style.

" At last at God's good pleasure arrived John Willock the second time from Embden ; whose return was so joyful to the brethren that their zeal and godly courage daily increased. And, albeit he contracted a dangerous sickness, yet he ceased not from labours, but taught and exhorted from his bed : some of the nobility (of whom some are fallen back, amongst whom the Lord Seaton is chief), with many barons and gentlemen, were his auditors, and by him were godly instructed and wondrously comforted. They kept their conventions and held counsels with such gravity and closeness that the enemies trembled. The images were stolen away in all parts of the country ; and in Edinburgh was that great idol called Saint Giles first drowned in the North Loch, afterwards burnt, which raised no small trouble in the town. For, the friars croaking [1] like ravens upon the bishops, the bishops ran upon the Queen, who to them was favourable enough, but that she thought it could not stand with her advantage to offend such a multitude as then took upon them the defence of the Evangel and the name of Protestants. And yet consented she to summon the preachers ; whereat the Protestants, neither offended nor yet thereof afraid, determined to keep the day of summons ; as that they did. Which perceived by the prelates and priests, they procured a proclamation to be publicly made, that all men who were come to the town without commandment of the authority

[1] " rowping."

8

should with all diligence repair to the Borders and there remain fifteen days; for the Bishop of Galloway, in this manner of rhyme, said to the Queen :

> Madame, because they are come without order,
> I red ye, send them to the Border.

" Now so had God provided that the quarter of the West-land (in the which were many faithful men) was that same day returned from the Border ; who, understanding the matter to proceed from the malice of the priests, assembled themselves together, and made passage to themselves, till they came to the very privy chamber, where the Queen Regent and the bishops were. The gentlemen began to complain upon their strange entertainment, considering that her Grace had found in them so faithful obedience in all things lawful. While the Queen began to craft, a zealous and a bold man, James Chalmers of Gadgirth, said : ' Madam, we know that this is the malice and device of these knaves and of that bastard (meaning the Bishop of St. Andrews) that stands by you. We avow to God, we shall make a day of it. They oppress us and our tenants for feeding of their idle bellies ; they trouble our preachers and would murder them and us. Shall we suffer this any longer ? No, Madam, it shall not be.' And therewith every

man put on his steel bonnet. There was heard
nothing of the Queen's part but ' My joys, my
hearts, what ails you? Me [1] means no evil to you
or your preachers. The bishops shall do you
no wrong. Ye are all my loving subjects. Me
knew nothing of this proclamation. The day of
your preachers shall be discharged, and me will
hear the controversy that is between the bishops
and you. They shall do you no wrong.' ' My
lords,' she said to the bishops, ' I forbid you
either to trouble them or their preachers.' And
unto the gentlemen, who were wonderfully com-
moved, she turned again and said, ' O my hearts,
should ye not love the Lord your God with all
your heart, with all your mind, and should ye
not love your neighbours as yourselves?' With
these and the like fair words she kept the bishops
from buffets at that time.

" And so, the day of summons being discharged,
began the brethren universal to be further encouraged. But yet could the bishops in no sort
be quiet; for, Saint Giles' day approaching, they
gave charge to the Provost, Baillies and Council
of Edinburgh, either to get again the old Saint
Giles or else upon their expense to make a new
image. The Council answered that to them the

[1] Frenchwoman's pigeon English.

charge appeared very unjust; for they understood that God in some places had commanded idols and images to be destroyed; but where He had commanded images to be set up they had not read, and desired the bishop to find a warrant for his commandment. Whereat the bishop offended, admonished under pain of cursing; which they prevented by a formal appellation, appealing from him, as from a partial and corrupt judge, unto the Pope's Holiness; and so, greater things shortly following, that passed into oblivion.

"Yet would not the priests and friars cease to have that solemnity and manifest abomination which they usually had upon Saint Giles' day; to wit, they would have that idol borne; and, therefore, was all preparation necessary duly made. A marmoset idol was borrowed from the Grey Friars (a silver piece of James Carmichael was laid in pledge). It was fast fixed with iron nails upon a barrow called the fertor. There assembled priests, friars, canons, and rotten papists, with tabrets and trumpets, banners and bagpipes; and who was there to lead the ring but the Queen Regent herself with all her shavelings for honour of that feast! West about goes it and comes down the High Street, and down to the Canoncross. The Queen Regent

dined that day in Sandie Carpetyne's house between the Bows ; and so, when the idol returned
back again, she left it and passed in to her dinner.

" The hearts of the brethren were wonderfully
inflamed, and, seeing such abomination manifestly
maintained, were decreed to be revenged. They
were divided into several companies, whereof not
one knew of another. There were some temporisers
that day (amongst whom David Forres, called the
General, was one), who, fearing the chance to be
done as it fell, laboured to stay the brethren.
But that could not be ; for, immediately after that
the Queen was entered in the lodging, some of
those that were of the enterprise drew near to the
idol, as willing to help to bear him, and, getting
the fertor upon their shoulders, began to shudder,
that thereby the idol should have fallen. But that
was prevented by the iron nails, as we have said ;
and so began one to cry, ' Down with the idol !
down with it ! ' And so without delay it was
pulled down. Some brag made the priests' patrons
at the first ; but, when they saw the feebleness
of their god—for one took him by the heels, and,
thumping [1] his head to the causeway, left Dagon
without head or hands, and said, ' Fie upon thee,
thou young Saint Giles, thy father would have

[1] " dadding."

tarried for such '—this considered (we say) the priests and friars fled faster than they did at Pinkie Cleuch. There might have been seen so sudden a fray as seldom has been seen among that sort of men within this realm ; for down go the crosses, off go the surplices. The Grey Friars gaped, the Black Friars blew, the priests panted and fled, and happy was he that first got to the house ; for such a sudden fray came never amongst the generation of Antichrist within this realm before." [1]

The second extract also deals with a tumult of the old religion :—

" How the servant of God was entreated, and what he did from the day that he entered within the Sea-tower of Saint Andrews, which was in the end of January in the year of God 1546, unto the first of March the same year, when he suffered, we cannot certainly tell, except we understand that he wrote somewhat being in prison ; but that was suppressed by the enemies. The Cardinal delayed no time, but caused all bishops, yea, all the clergy that had any preeminence to be called to Saint Andrews against the penult of February, that consultation might be had on that question which in his mind was no less resolved than Christ's death

[1] *History*, i. 256 ff.

was in the mind of Caiaphas ; but, that the rest
should bear the like burden with him, he would
that they should before the world subscribe whatsoever he did. In that day was wrought no less
a wonder than was at the accusation and death
of Jesus Christ, when that Pilate and Herod, who
before were enemies, were made friends by con-
senting of them both to Christ's condemnation ;
differing nothing except that Pilate and Herod
were brethren, under their father the Devil, in the
estate called temporal, and these two of whom we
are to speak were brethren, sons under the same
father the Devil, in the estate ecclesiastical. If we
interlace merriness with earnest matters, pardon us,
good reader ; for the fact is so notable that it
deserveth long memory.

"The Cardinal was known proud ; and Dunbar,
Archbishop of Glasgow, was known a glorious fool ;
and yet, because he was called sometimes the King's
Master, he was Chancellor of Scotland. The
Cardinal comes even this same year, in the end
of harvest before, to Glasgow ; upon what purpose
we omit. But, while they remain together, the one
in the town the other in the Castle, question rises
for bearing of their crosses. The Cardinal alleged,
by reason of his cardinalship, that he was *Legatus
Natus* and Primate within Scotland in the kingdom

of Antichrist, that he should have the preeminence, and that his cross should not only go before, but that also it should only be borne wheresoever he was. Good Gukstoun Glaikstour, the foresaid Archbishop, lacked no reasons, as he thought, for maintenance of his glory : he was an Archbishop in his own diocese and in his own cathedral-seat and church, and therefore ought to give place to no man. The power of the Cardinal was but begged from Rome, and appertained but to his own person and not to his bishopric ; for it might be that his successor should not be cardinal ; but his dignity was annexed with his office, and did appertain to all that ever should be Bishops of Glasgow. Howsoever these doubts were resolved by the doctors of divinity of both the prelates, yet the decision was as ye shall hear. Coming forth (or going in, all is one) at the choir-door of Glasgow Kirk, begins striving for state between the two cross-bearers, so that from glooming they come to shouldering ; from shouldering they go to buffets, and from dry blows to fists and fisticuffs ; and then, for charity's sake, they cry, *Dispersit, dedit pauperibus*, and essay which of the crosses was finest metal, which staff was strongest, and which bearer could best defend his master's preeminence ; and, that there should be no superiority on that behalf, to the ground go both the crosses. And then began no little fray, but yet a merry game; for rochets were rent, tippets were torn, crowns were knapped, and side-gowns might have been seen wantonly wag from one wall to the other. Many of them lacked beards, and that was the more pity, and, therefore, could not buckle other by the hair,[1] as bold men would have done. But fie on the jackmen, that did not their duty; for, had the one part of them rencountered the other, then had all gone right. But the sanctuary, we suppose, saved the lives of many. How merrily that ever this be written, it was bitter mirth[2] to the Cardinal and his court. It was more than irregularity; yea, it might well have been judged *lèse majesté* to the son of perdition, the Pope's own person; and yet the other, in his folly as proud as a peacock, would let the Cardinal know that he was a bishop, when the other was but Beaton, before he got Aberbrothock. This enmity was judged mortal and without all hope of reconciliation."[3]

[1] " byrse."
[2] "bowrding."
[3] *History*, i. 144 ff.

## CHAPTER II.

### HIS RELIGIOUS CONVICTIONS

HAVING enumerated the works of the Reformer, we proceed to sketch the religious and political principles embodied in them.

Much of the work he had to do was destructive. He had to sweep out of the minds of men a whole world of superstitions, and out of the country masses of superstitious usages, founded on these false opinions. This part of his task Knox performed with zest, employing all the powers of sarcasm and invective, of which he was a master, in turning the old Church into ridicule. Of ecclesiastical lore he cannot be claimed to have possessed very much; but his stores were ample to overwhelm the feeble opponents who entered the field against him. In his very first sermon at St. Andrews he boldly maintained that the Pope was Antichrist. "And then began he to decipher the lives of diverse popes and the lives of all the shavelings for the most

part ; their doctrine and laws he plainly proved
to repugn directly to the doctrine and laws of God
the Father and of Christ Jesus His Son." And,
in a petition to Parliament in 1560, which he drew
up in the name of the barons, gentlemen, burgesses,
and others, professing the Lord Jesus Christ within
the realm of Scotland, he thus sketched in brief
but pregnant terms the evils of the time :

"And, first, seeing that God, of His great mercy
by the light of His Word, has manifested to no small
number of this realm, that the doctrine of the
Roman Kirk, received by the said clergy and
maintained through their tyranny by fire and sword,
contained in itself many pestiferous errors, which
cannot but bring damnation to the souls of such
as therewith shall be infected—such as are the
doctrine of transubstantiation ; of the adoration of
Christ's body under the form of bread as they term
it ; of the merits of works, and justification that
they allege comes thereby ; together with the doctrine
of papistical indulgences, purgatory, pilgrimage, and
praying to departed saints ; which are all either
repugnant to the plain Scriptures or else have no
ground in the doctrine of our Master Jesus Christ,
His prophets nor apostles—we humbly, therefore,
crave of your honours, that such doctrine and
idolatry as by God's Word are condemned, so may

they be abolished by act of this present parliament, and punishment appointed for the transgressors.

"Secondly, seeing that the sacraments of Jesus Christ are most shamefully abused and profaned by that Roman harlot and her sworn vassals; and also because the true discipline of the ancient Kirk is now utterly extinguished among that sect: for who within the realm are more corrupt in life and manners than are they that are called the clergy, doing all abomination without fear of punishment? we humbly, therefore, desire your Honours to find remedy against the one and the other.

"Thirdly, because that Man of Sin often most falsely claims to himself the titles of 'the vicar of Christ'; 'the successor of Peter'; 'the head of the Kirk'; 'that he cannot err'; 'that all power is granted unto him,' etc., by the which usurped authority he takes upon him the distribution and possession of the whole patrimony of the Kirk, whereby the true ministers of the Word of God long time have been utterly neglected, godly learning despised, schools not provided, and the poor not only defrauded of their portion, but also tyrannously oppressed; we likewise hereof desire remedy." [1]

The superstition of the age culminated in the doctrine and practice of the Mass, against which

[1] *Works*, ii. 90.

accordingly Knox directed the whole force of his artillery. Early in his career, in a discourse already mentioned, in the presence of the clergy of the North of England, he maintained the thesis that ⊤ the Mass is idolatry ; and, throughout his subsequent activity, he never hesitated to apply to this practice all the fulminations against idolatry to be found in the Scriptures. Thus, in the preface to his report of his disputation with the Abbot of Crossraguel, he paraphrases the ironical description of the making of an idol found in the prophecy of Isaiah, in the following terms :—

" The prophet, in description of their vanities, saith, ' The earth bringeth forth the tree, it groweth by moisture and natural humidity,[1] it is cut down by the hand of the hewer. A part thereof is burnt, a part spent in uses necessary to man, another part chosen to be made an idol. This is formed to the likeness of man or woman, and then set up and worshipped as a god.' All these and some more shall we find to assist and concur in the making of this great god of bread. The wheat is sown and nourished in the earth ; rain, dew and heat bring it to maturity ; the reaper or shearer cutteth it down ; the cart or sledge, drawn by horse or some other beast, draweth it to the barn

[1] " wacknes."

or to the barnyard ; the tasker or the foot of the
ox treadeth it out ; the fan delivereth it from the
chaff; the miller and the millstones, by the help
of wind or water, make it to be meal ; the smith
maketh the irons that give to that god his length
and breadth, likeness and form ; the fine substance
of that god is neither wood, gold nor silver, but
water and meal made in manner of a bannock [1] ;
and then must the workmen take good heed to
their hand, for, if the fire be too hot, that god's
skin must be burnt; if the irons be ill cleaned,[2]
his face will be blacked ; if, in making the roundness,
the ring be broken, then must another of his fellows
receive that honour to be made a god ; and the
creased or cracked miserable cake, that once was
in hope to be made a god, must be given to a
baby to play him withal.  And yet is not all the
danger past ; for, if there be not an anointed priest
to play his part aright, all the former artificers
have lost their labour, for without him that god
cannot be made : yea, if he have not intention to
consecrate, the fashioned god remaineth bread, and
so the blind people commit idolatry.

"These are the artificers and workmen that
travail in making of this god : I think as many

---

[1] "drammock."
[2] "evil dight."

in number as the prophet reciteth to have travailed in the making of the idols ; and, if the power of both shall be compared, I think they shall be found in all things equal, except that the god of bread is subject unto more dangers than were the idols of the Gentiles. Men made them : men make it. They were deaf and dumb : it cannot speak, hear nor see. Briefly, in infirmity they wholly agree, except that, as I have said, the poor god of bread is most miserable of all other idols ; for, according to their matter whereof they are made, they will remain without corruption many years ; but within one year that god will putrify, and then he must be burnt. They can abide the vehemency of the wind, frost, rain or snow ; but the wind will blow that god to the sea, the rain or the snow will make it dough again ; yea, which is most of all to be feared, that god is a prey, if he be not well kept, to rats and mice ; for they will desire no better dinner than white round gods enough. But oh then, what becometh of Christ's natural body ? By miracle it flies to the heaven again, if the papists teach truly ; for, how soon soever the mouse takes hold, so soon flieth Christ away and letteth her gnaw the bread. A bold and puissant mouse, but a feeble and miserable god ! Yet would I ask a question : Whether hath the

priest or the mouse greater power ? By his words
it is made a god ; by her teeth it ceaseth to be
a god : let them advise and then answer.

"If any think that I ought not to mock that which
the world so long hath holden, and great princes
yet hold in so great veneration, I answer, that not
only I, but also all godly ought not only to mock
but also to curse and detest whatsoever is not God
and yet usurpeth the name, power and honour of
God ; and also that we ought both to mock, gainsay
and abhor all religion obtruded on the people without assurance of God and His Word, having neither
respect to antiquity, to multitude, to authority,
nor estimation of them that maintain the same." [1]

The language of Knox in controversy sounds
in our ears rude and exaggerated ; as, indeed, the
relics of bygone polemics are usually the reverse
of admirable to posterity. But the defence of
Luther is worth recalling : " Do not think," he
wrote to Spalatin, "that the Gospel can be advanced
without tumult, trouble and uproar. You cannot
make a pen of a sword; and the Word of God is
a sword. It is war, overthrow, trouble, destruction,
poison. It meets the children of Ephraim, as Amos
says, like a bear on the road or like a lioness in
the wood." The state of Europe with which the

[1] *Works*, vi. 171 ff.

Reformers had to contend is sheltered from modern
criticism by the very excess of its own corruption ;
and, even in the foregoing extracts, words and clauses
have had to be suppressed. Those who know
best what the moral condition of Scotland was
before the Reformation, as this is revealed in her
literature—for example, in the writings of the poets
Dunbar and Lindsay—are the most likely to be
thankful to Knox for the changes he introduced
into the country. Had he done nothing more than
what he did to promote decency, he would have
deserved the eternal gratitude of Scotsmen.

The weapon with which Knox fought this battle
was the Word of God. This was the fan with
which he "throughly purged" the floor of the
Church. In his first sermon at St. Andrews he
showed that the Church is the pillar of the eternal
verity only because it hears the voice of its own
pastor, Jesus Christ, and will not listen to a stranger.
And, from this point onwards to the very close
of his career, he kept on repeating, in every form
in which it could be expressed, that nothing is
lawful in the Church which is not found in the
Word of God. This may be called his master
principle ; and he is never tired of repeating it.
Others were content with holding that nothing

could be admitted into the Church which was forbidden in the Bible; but Knox went much farther,
demanding a positive sanction out of Scripture for
everything which he would admit. Not only did
this work havoc with the ecclesiastical system of
Rome, but it led him to attribute to the Church of
England a considerable share of what he called "the
dregs of papistry." "Man," he remarks, "always
thinks he can devise a more perfect honouring of
God than that which Himself hath commanded.
Witness the Israelites in the desert, the Ten Tribes
under Jeroboam, the Pharisees and the rest of the
sects in Christ's time; and the papists before and
in our own time. For, let any of them be demanded,
How know ye that these your works, rites and ceremonies please God, seeing ye have not His commandment to do the same? straight they shall
answer, 'They are laudable, they are honest and
decent, they have good significations, they pleased
our fathers, and the most part of the world has
used the same.' And thus into idolatry the corrupt
children follow the footsteps of their fathers."

None of the other Reformers went so far in
confining the arrangements of the Church to what
is actually prescribed in the Scriptures. Even
Calvin was appealed to, on one occasion, against
Knox's severity; and the Swiss Reformer wrote

to him : " In regard to ceremonies, I trust that
your strictness, although it may displease many,
will be regulated by discretion. We should,
indeed, do our endeavour that the Church may
be purged of all the defilements which flowed from
error and superstition. We should also earnestly
strive that the mysteries of God be not polluted
by absurd and unmeaning mixtures. With this
exception, you know well that certain things, though
not positively approved, must be tolerated." The
Westminster Confession of Faith, while frequently
laying stress on the principle that the Bible is
the sole authority in the Church, yet acknowledges
that " there are some circumstances concerning the
worship of God and government of the Church,
common to human actions and societies, which are
to be ordered by the light of nature and Christian
prudence, according to the general rules of the
Word, which are always to be observed " ; and
this could be converted into a pretty wide door
for the admission of innovations. The principle
laid down by Knox, although upon the whole a
wholesome one, is not easy to carry through ; and
it may be doubted if even he was invariably true
to it. Let anyone read the Order of the General
Fast,[1] appointed by the General Assembly in 1565,

[1] *Works*, vi. 391.

and he will probably acknowledge that, in spite of the appeals in it to Scripture, the ceremony there so minutely prescribed had not only no direct Scriptural warrant, but was contrary to the spirit of the New Testament.

But the Bible was to Knox not only thus a law to regulate ceremonies and a fan with which to purge out the excesses of the Roman superstition : he wielded it, besides, as a tool for building up the spiritual Jerusalem ; and it was obviously from the heart that he said, " I delight in nothing so much as in the simple and native meaning of the Scriptures, as they be alleged in their own places by the Holy Ghost." [1]   It is much to be regretted that more of his sermons have not come down to us ; because in them we should in all probability have discovered the secret of the sway he exerted over his countrymen, and especially over the citizens of Edinburgh, who loved him because, like a good shepherd, he led them week by week into the green pastures and beside the still waters of the Word of God.   As far as the evidence available goes, he seems to have been specially a preacher of the Old Testament.   We do not find him, like Luther, wandering often among the flowery and fragrant meadows of the Gospels, expounding the miracles

[1] *Works*, v. 262.

and the parables of our Lord ; nor does he display
the exegetical precision of Calvin, who habitually
makes the historical and grammatical meaning of
a text the basis of the practical application. For
this Knox has not patience. He hurries quickly
from the exposition to the application ; the text
being only a point of departure for an expatiation
of his own ; and it does not seem to matter
much which text he chooses. Still, he possesses a
marvellous faculty for taking a book of the Old
Testament, or a portion of the Old Testament
history, and laying it alongside of the contemporary
history of his own country in such a way as to
bring out comparisons and contrasts, which illuminate the situation and reveal the path of duty. He
indulges little in apologies for the authority of the
Bible. The business of his life was to break down
the authority of Rome ; but those against whom
his polemic was directed acknowledged as well as
he the authority of Scripture ; so that there was no
need to waste time on the proof of that which was
conceded. It was later in the history of the Church
before theologians found it necessary to buttress the
authority of the Bible with elaborate evidences.
Even for Calvin, a much more systematic thinker,
the necessity for proving the authority of the
Scriptures hardly exists ; at least, he is satisfied with

the witness of the Spirit in the Scriptures speaking
to the spirit in the minds of the godly.

There is every reason to believe that the attachment of Knox to the Word of God was personal
and not merely professional. In the account of
his death-bed it comes out that he was in the habit
of reading the Book of Psalms once a month ; and
there breathes a heartfelt sincerity through his allusions to the Word of God in general. Nowhere is
this more fully expressed than in a letter which he
left behind him to the friends of reform in Scotland,
when closing his momentous visit in 1556 ; and this
document throws so much light on the primitive
conditions in which Christianity then existed in
Scotland that I shall quote the whole, which might
almost be an extract from the Acts of the Apostles :—

"A most wholesome counsel how to behave
ourselves in the midst of this wicked generation,
touching the daily exercise of God's most Holy
and Sacred Word.

"The Comfort of the Holy Ghost, etc., for
salutation.

"Not so much to instruct you as to leave with
you, dearly beloved brethren, some testimony of
my love, I have thought good to communicate with
you, in these few lines, my weak counsel, how I
would ye should behave yourselves, in the midst

of this wicked generation, touching the exercise of God's most sacred and holy Word, without which neither shall knowledge increase, godliness appear, nor fervency continue amongst you. For, as the Word of God is the beginning of life spiritual, without which all flesh is dead in God's presence, and the lantern to our feet, without the brightness whereof all the posterity of Adam doth walk in darkness, and as it is the foundation of faith, without which no man understandeth the goodwill of God, so it is also the only organ and instrument which God useth to strengthen the weak, to comfort the afflicted, to reduce to mercy by repentance such as have erred, and, finally, to preserve and keep the very life of the soul in all assaults and temptations. And thereof, if that ye desire your knowledge to be increased, your faith to be confirmed, your conscience to be quieted and comforted or, finally, your soul to be preserved in life, let your exercise be frequent in the law of your Lord God. Despise not that precept which Moses, who by his own experience had learned what comfort lieth hid within the Word of God, gave to the Israelites in these words : ' These words, which I command thee this day, shall be in thy heart : and thou shalt exercise thy children in them. Thou shalt talk of them when thou art at home in thy house, and as thou walkest by the way, and when thou liest down, and when thou risest up ; and thou shalt bind them for a sign upon thy hand, and they shall be papers of remembrance between thine eyes ; and thou shalt write them upon the posts of thy house and upon thy gates.' And Moses in another place commandeth them to ' remember the law of the Lord God, to do it, that it may be well with them and with their children in the land which the Lord their God should give them,' meaning, that, like as frequent memory and repetition of God's precepts is the means whereby the fear of God, which is the beginning of all wisdom and felicity, is kept recent in mind, so is negligence and oblivion of God's benefits received the first degree of defection from God.

" Now, if the Law, which by reason of our weakness can work nothing but wrath and anger, was so effectual that, remembered and rehearsed of purpose to do it, it brought to the people a corporal benediction, what shall we say that the glorious Gospel of Christ Jesus doth work, so that with reverence it be entreated ? St. Paul calleth it the sweet odour of life to those that shall receive life, borrowing his similitude of odoriferous herbs or precious ointments, whose nature is, the more that they be touched or moved, to send forth their odour more pleasant and delectable. Even such, dear brethren, is the blessed Evangel of our Lord Jesus ; for, the more that it be entreated, the more comfortable and puissant it is to such as do hear, read or exercise the same. I am not ignorant, that, as the Israelites loathed the manna, because that every day they saw and ate but one thing, so some there be now-a-days (who will not be held of the worst sort) that, after once reading some parcels of the Scriptures, do commit themselves altogether to profane authors and human lectures, because that the variety of matters therein contained doth bring with it daily delectation, where contrariwise within the simple Scriptures of God the perpetual repetition of one thing is troublesome and wearisome. This temptation, I confess, may enter in God's very elect for a time ; but impossible it is that therein they continue to the end ; for God's election, besides other evident signs, hath this ever joined with it, that God's elect are called from ignorance (I speak of those that are come to the years of knowledge) to some taste and feeling of God's mercy, of the which they are never so satisfied in this life but from time to time they hunger and they thirst to eat the bread that descended from heaven and to drink the water that springeth to life everlasting ; which they cannot

do but by the means of faith, and faith looketh
ever to the will of God revealed by the Word,
so that faith hath both her beginning and continuance by the Word of God. And so I say, that
impossible it is that God's chosen children can
despise or reject the word of their salvation of any
long continuance, neither yet loathe it to the end.

" Often it is that God's elect are held in such
bondage and thraldom, that they cannot have the
bread of life broken unto them, neither yet free
liberty to exercise themselves in God's holy Word ;
but then God's dear children do not loathe, but most
gladly do they covet the food of their souls ; then
do they accuse their former negligence, then lament
they the miserable affliction of their brethren, and
then cry and call they in their hearts (and openly
where they dare) for free passage of the Gospel.
This hunger and thirst doth prove the life of their
souls. But, if such men as having liberty to read
and exercise themselves in God's holy Scriptures
yet begin to weary, because from time to time
they read but one thing, I ask, Why weary they
not also every day to eat bread ? every day to
drink wine ? every day to behold the brightness
of the sun ? and to use the rest of God's creatures,
which every day do keep their own substance,
course and nature ? They shall answer, I trust,

Because such creatures have a strength, as oft as they are used, to expel hunger, to quench thirst, to restore strength, and to preserve the life. O miserable creatures! who dare attribute more power and strength to the corruptible creatures in nourishing and preserving the mortal carcase than to the eternal Word of God in nourishment of the soul, which is immortal! To reason with their damnable unthankfulness at this present it is not my purpose : but to you, dear brethren, I write my knowledge and do speak my conscience, that, so necessary as the use of meat and drink is to the preservation of life corporal, and so necessary as the heat and brightness of the sun is to the quickening of herbs, and to expel darkness, so necessary is also to the life everlasting, and to the illumination and light of the soul, the perpetual meditation, exercise and use of God's holy Word.

"And therefore, dear brethren, if that ye look for a life to come, of necessity it is that ye exercise yourselves in the book of the Lord your God. Let no day slip over without some comfort received from the mouth of God. Open your ears, and He will speak even pleasant things to your heart. Close not your eyes, but diligently let them behold what portion of substance is left to you within your Father's testament. Let your tongues learn to praise the gracious goodness of Him whose mere mercy hath called you from darkness to light, and from death to life. Neither yet may ye do this so quietly that ye will admit no witness. No, brethren, ye are ordained of God to rule your own houses in His true fear and according to His Word. Within your own houses, I say, in some cases, ye are bishops and kings; your wife, children, servants and family are your bishopric and charge; of you it shall be required how carefully and diligently ye have always instructed them in God's true knowledge, how that ye have studied in them to plant virtue and repress vice. And therefore, I say, ye must make them partakers in reading, exhorting, and in making common prayers, which I would in every house were used once a day at least. But above all things, dear brethren, study to practise in life that which the Word of God commandeth, and then be assured that ye shall never hear nor read the same without fruit. And thus much for the exercises within your house.

"Considering that St. Paul calleth the congregation 'the body of Christ,' whereof every one of us is a member, teaching us thereby that no member is of sufficiency to sustain and feed itself without the help and support of another, I think it necessary, for the conference of Scriptures, assemblies of brethren to be had. The order therein to be observed is expressed by St. Paul, and therefore need not I to use many words in that behalf; only expressing my wish, that, when ye convene or come together—which I would were once a week—that your beginning should be from confession of your offences and invocation of the Spirit of the Lord Jesus to assist you in all your godly enterprises. And then let some place of Scripture be plainly and distinctly read, so much as shall be thought sufficient for one day or time; which ended, if any brother have exhortation, question or doubt, let him not fear to speak or move the same, so that he do it with moderation, either to edify or to be edified. And hereof I doubt not great profit shall shortly ensue; for, first, by hearing, reading and conferring the Scriptures in the assembly, the whole body of the Scriptures of God shall become familiar, the judgments and spirits of men shall be tried, their patience and modesty shall be known, and, finally, their gifts and utterance shall appear. Multiplication of words, prolix interpretations, and wilfulness in reasoning are to be avoided at all times and in all places, but chiefly in the congregation, where nothing ought to be respected except the glory of God and comfort or edification of brethren.

" If anything occur within the text, or else arise in reasoning, which your judgments cannot resolve or your capacities apprehend, let the same be noted and put in writing, before ye dismiss the congregation, that, when God shall offer unto you any interpreter, your doubts, being noted and known, may have the more expedient resolution ; or else that, when ye shall have occasion to write to such as with whom ye would communicate your judgments, your letters may signify and declare your unceasing desire that ye have of God and of His true religion ; and they, I doubt not, according to their talents, will endeavour and bestow their faithful labours to satisfy your godly petitions. Of myself I will speak as I think : I will more gladly spend fifteen hours in communicating my judgment with you, in explaining as God pleases to open to me any place of Scripture, than half an hour in any other matter.

" Further, I would, in reading the Scripture ye should join some books of the Old and some of the New Testament together, as Genesis and one of the Evangelists, Exodus with another, and so forth ; ever ending such books as ye begin (as the time will suffer), for it will greatly comfort you to hear that harmony and well-tuned song of the Holy Spirit speaking to our fathers from the beginning.

It shall confirm you in these dangerous and perilous days to behold the face of Christ's loving Spouse and Church, from Abel to Himself and from Himself to this day, in all ages to be one. Be frequent in the Prophets and in the Epistles of St. Paul, for the multitude of matters, most comfortable therein contained, requireth exercise and good memory. Like as your assemblies ought to begin with confession and invocation of God's Holy Spirit, so would I that they were finished with thanksgiving and common prayers for princes, rulers and magistrates ; for the liberty and free passage of Christ's Evangel ; for the comfort and deliverance of our afflicted brethren in all places now persecuted, but most cruelly within the realms of France and England ; and for such other things as the Spirit of the Lord Jesus shall teach unto you to be profitable either to yourselves or to your brethren, wheresover they be.

" If thus (or better) I shall hear that ye exercise yourselves, dear brethren, then will I praise God for your great obedience, as for them that have not only received the Word of grace with gladness but that also, with care and diligence, do keep the same as a treasure and jewel most precious. And, because that I cannot suspect that ye will do the contrary at this present, I will use no threatenings ; for my good hope is, that ye shall walk as the sons of light in the midst of this wicked generation ; that ye shall be as stars in the night season, who yet are not changed into darkness; that ye shall be as wheat among the cockle, and yet that ye shall not change your nature, which ye have received by grace through the fellowship and participation which we have with the Lord Jesus in His body and blood ; and, finally, that ye shall be of the number of the prudent virgins, daily renewing your lamps with oil, as they that patiently do abide the glorious apparition and coming of the Lord Jesus ; whose omnipotent Spirit rule and instruct, illuminate and comfort your hearts and minds in all assaults now and ever. Amen.

" The grace of the Lord Jesus rest with you.

" Remember my weakness in your daily prayers. The 7th of July, 1556.

" Your Brother unfeigned,

" JOHN KNOX." [1]

While the authority of the Word of God is one of the pillars of the Reformation, it is usually stated that the doctrine of Justification by Faith is the other. And it is worthy of note that Knox's very first publication was a treatise on this important

[1] *Works*, iv. 129 ff.

subject, penned, however, not by himself, but by a fellow-exile, during the period of his imprisonment in France. Knox appears to consider it a commendation of this production that it came from the pen of "no speculative theologue," but from that of a simple layman ; and at any rate the clearness and force of the exposition are now interesting evidences of the grip with which at that time this doctrine had laid hold of the general mind. At the request of the author, Henry Balnaves, Knox digested it into chapters, to which he appended summaries, together with a table of contents. This was a friendly action, thoroughly well done ; although even these additions of Knox fail to give the work much distinction ; and we cannot help regretting that he did not write on the subject himself.

One qualification for so doing he possessed in a remarkable degree. It is the poignant and intolerable sense of sin that makes the soul cling to the cross of Christ. It was by this experience that both St. Paul and Luther were prepared for appreciating the righteousness of God, after they had realised that their guilt was too great to be atoned-for by anything that they could do themselves. The conscience of Knox was preternaturally tender. How this peculiarity was originally

produced in him we do not know ; but the probability is, that it was due to experiences of
conviction of sin and of hopeless struggle after
righteousness, similar to those of St. Paul and
Luther, belonging to the early period of which
we possess no record ; and in his subsequent life
it can have been developed only by a careful walk
with God and a constant comparison of his own
conduct and character with the perfect model of
the Bible.

Often he accuses himself, in most touching terms,
of shortcomings in the discharge of his ministry,
and even of fear in the face of danger—the last
thing which any other person would have thought
of laying to his charge. Here is a searching review
of his ministry in England, which will be read by
everyone engaged in work of the same kind with
sympathy :—

" The ministers who were the distributers of this
bread, the true Word of God, wherewith the
multitude within England was fed, lacked not their
offences, which also moved God to send us to the
sea. And, because the offences of no man are so
manifest unto me as are mine own, only of myself
I will be the accuser.

" It is not unknown unto many, that I (the most
wretched) was one of that number whom **God**

appointed to receive that bread, as it was broken by Christ Jesus, to distribute and give the same to such as He had called to this banquet, in that part of His table where He appointed me to serve. It is not in my knowledge nor judgment to define nor determine what portion or quantity every man received of this bread, neither yet how that which they received agreed with their stomachs. But of this I am assured, that the benediction of Christ Jesus so multiplied the portion that I received of His hands, that during that banquet (this I write to the praise of His name and to the accusation of mine own unthankfulness) the bread never failed when the hungry soul craved or cried for food ; and at the end of the banquet, mine own conscience beareth witness, that my hands gathered up the crumbs that were left in such abundance, that my basket was full among the rest.

" To be plain, mine own conscience beareth record to myself, how small was my learning, and how weak I was of judgment, when Christ Jesus called me to be His steward ; and how mightily, day by day and time by time, He multiplied His graces with me, if I should conceal, I were most wicked and unthankful.

" But alas ! how blinded was my heart, and how little I did consider the dignity of that office, and

the power of God that then multiplied and blessed
the bread which the people received of my hands,
this day mine own conscience beareth witness to
myself. God I take to record in my conscience,
that I delivered the same bread that I received of
Christ's hands, and that I mixed no poison with
the same ; that is, I taught Christ's Gospel without
any mixture of men's dreams, devices or fantasies.
But alas! I did not with such fervency, with such
indifferency, and with such diligence, as this day
I know my duty was to have done.

"Some complained in those days, that the preachers
were indiscreet persons ; yea, and some called them
railers, and worse, because they spake against the
manifest iniquity of men, and especially of those
that were then placed in authority as well in the
court as in other offices universally throughout the
realm, both in cities, towns and villages. And
among other, peradventure, my rude plainness dis-
pleased some, who did complain that rashly I
did speak of men's faults ; so that all men might
know and perceive of whom I meant. But alas!
this day my conscience accuseth me, that I spake
not so plainly as my duty was to have done ;
for I ought to have said to the wicked man expressly
by his name, 'Thou shalt die the death.' For
I find Jeremy the prophet to have done so to

Pashur the high priest and to Zedekiah the king ; and not only him, but also Elijah, Elisha, Micah, Amos, Daniel, Christ Jesus Himself, and after Him His Apostles, expressly to have named the blood-thirsty tyrants, abominable idolaters and dissembling hypocrites of their days. If that we the preachers within the realm of England were appointed by God to be the salt of the earth, as His other messengers were before us, alas! why held we back the salt where manifest corruption did appear? (I accuse none but myself.) The blind love that I did bear to this my wicked carcase was the chief cause that I was not fervent and faithful enough in that behalf ; for I had no will to provoke the hatred of all men against me, and therefore so touched I the vices of men in the presence of the greatest, that they might see themselves to be offenders. I dare not say that I was the greatest flatterer, but yet, nevertheless, I would not be seen to proclaim manifest war against the manifest wicked : whereof unfeignedly I ask my God mercy.

" As I was not so fervent in rebuking manifest iniquity as it became me to have been, so was I not so indifferent [1] a feeder as is required of Christ's steward. For in preaching Christ's Gospel, albeit mine eye (as knoweth God) was not much upon

[1] Without respect of persons.

worldly promotion, yet the love of friends and carnal affection of some men with whom I was most familiar allured me to make more residence in one place than in another, having more respect to the pleasure of a few than to the necessity of many. That day I thought I had not sinned, if I had not been idle; but this day I know it was my duty to have had consideration how long I had remained in one place, and how many hungry souls were in other places to whom, alas! none took pain to break and distribute the bread of life.

"Moreover, remaining in one place, I was not so diligent as mine office required; but some time, by counsel of carnal friends, I spared the body; some time I spent in worldly business of particular friends; and some time in taking recreation and pastime by exercise of the body.

"And, albeit men may judge these to be light and small offences, yet I know and confess, that, unless pardon should to me be granted in Christ's blood, every one of these three offences aforenamed— that is to say, the lack of fervency in reproving sin, the lack of indifferency in feeding those that were hungry, and the lack of diligence in the execution of mine office—deserved damnation.

"And, beside these, I was assaulted, yea, infected and corrupted with more gross sins; that is, my wicked nature desired the favours, the estimation and praise of men ; against which, albeit that sometime the Spirit of God did move me to fight, and earnestly did stir me (God knoweth I lie not) to sob and lament for those imperfections, yet never ceased they to trouble me, when any occasion was offered. And so privily and craftily did they enter into my breast, that I could not perceive myself to be wounded, till vainglory had almost got the upperhand.

"O Lord ! be merciful to my great offence, and deal not with me according to my great iniquity, but, according to the multitude of Thy mercies, remove from me the burden of my sin ; for, of purpose and mind to have avoided the vain displeasure of man, I spared little to offend Thy Godly Majesty." [1]

But the most pathetic of all such utterances is contained in the last of his publications, his *Answer to a Letter of James Tyrie, a Scottish Jesuit*, written the year in which he died. It appears, indeed, to have been penned at an earlier date ; but we cannot do wrong in looking upon it as expressing the habitual attitude of his spirit to God all through his life :—

"Lord Jesus, receive my spirit, and put an end

[1] *Works*, iii. 268 ff.

at Thy good pleasure to this my miserable life ; for justice and truth are not to be found among the sons of men.

"JOHN KNOX with deliberate mind to his God.

" Be merciful unto me, O Lord, and call not into judgment my manifold sins, and chiefly those of which the world is not able to accuse me. In youth, mid-age, and now after many battles, I find nothing in me but vanity and corruption. For in quietness I am negligent, in trouble impatient, tending to desperation ; and in the mean state I am so carried away with vain fantasies that, alas ! O Lord, they withdraw me from the presence of Thy Majesty. Pride and ambition assault me on the one part, covetousness and malice trouble me on the other ; briefly, O Lord, the affections of the flesh do almost suppress the operation of Thy Spirit. I take Thee, O Lord, who only knowest the secrets of hearts, to record, that in none of the foresaid I do delight ; but that with them am I troubled, and that sore against the desire of my inward man, which sobs for my corruption, and would repose in Thy mercy alone ; to the which I claim, and that in the promise that Thou hast made to all penitent sinners, of whose number I profess myself to be one, in the obedience and death of my only Saviour, our Lord

Jesus Christ; in whom by Thy mere grace I doubt not myself to be elected to eternal salvation, whereof Thou hast given unto me, O Lord, most wretched and unthankful creature, most assured signs. For, being drowned in ignorance, Thou hast given unto me knowledge above the common sort of my brethren; my tongue hast Thou used to set forth Thy glory, to oppugn idolatry, error and false doctrine. Thou hast compelled me to forespeak as well deliverance to the afflicted as destruction to certain inobedient; the performance whereof not I alone, but the very blind world has already seen. But above all, O Lord, Thou, by the power of Thy Holy Spirit, hast sealed into my heart remission of sins, which I acknowledge and confess myself to have received by the precious blood of Jesus Christ once shed; by whose perfect obedience, I am assured, my manifold rebellions are defaced, my grievous sins purged, and my soul made the tabernacle of Thy Godly Majesty; Thou, O Father of mercies, Thy Son our Lord Jesus my only Saviour, Mediator and Advocate, and Thy Holy Spirit, remaining in the same by true faith; which is the only victory that overcometh the world.

"To Thee, therefore, O Lord, I commend my spirit; for I thirst to be resolved from this body of sin, and am assured that I shall rise again in

glory, howsoever it be that the wicked for a time
shall tread me and others Thy servants under their
feet.    Be merciful, O Lord, unto the Kirk within
this realm ; continue with it the light of Thy
Evangel ; augment the number of true preachers ;
and let Thy merciful providence look upon my
desolate bedfellow, the fruit of her bosom, and my
two dear children, Nathaniel and Eleazar.    Now,
Lord, put end to my miseries ! " [1]

In this extract it will be noted how, in spite
the depth and solemnity of the confession of sin,
the author nevertheless attains to the full assurance
of forgiveness ; and this truly evangelical note rings
out ever and anon in his writings, as it did no doubt
in his preaching.    Yet justification by faith does not
sing and dance in the very blood of Knox as it
did in Luther's.    In the German Reformer's company
we breathe an atmosphere of abounding freedom
and spiritual joy, to which the Scottish one only
occasionally attains ; and what held the latter down
was a conscience imperfectly emancipated.

The part of Balnaves' book which will probably
be most relished by the modern reader is the account
it gives of the life of justification, comprising plain
and sensible rules for the walk and conversation of a
Christian man.    In the debt which the world owes to

[1] *Works*, **vi.** 483.

the heroes of the religious revolution of the sixteenth century there is no item which would be paid with more gratitude, if it were thoroughly understood, than the new conception of good works with which they familiarised the mind of Europe. In preceding centuries good works had come to be understood more and more in an artificial sense. To go on pilgrimage, to endow a religious house, to become a monk, to fast or otherwise torture the body—these and the like were good works; and the very name "religious" was restricted, as it still is where the Romish system prevails, to persons who had left the world, with its every-day duties, and given themselves up to a life of contemplation. But Balnaves shows with quiet force that the good works with which God is well pleased are such as these : to be a good father, a good son, a good citizen, to be diligent in business, and to be in all respects a good specimen of manhood. This alteration of the point of view may be said to lie at the bottom of all the progress of the modern world. It is a mistake to suppose that the Reformation was mainly occupied with theological doctrines : it was even more a revolution in morals ; and Knox is excelled by none in honest zeal to enlighten the public conscience. " It is not enough," he says, " to justify us before God that civil laws cannot accuse us. Nay, brethren, the eye of our God pierceth deeper than man's law can stretch. The law of man cannot convict the earl, the lord, the baron or gentleman for oppressing the poor labourers of the ground; for his defence is ready, 'I may do with my own as best pleaseth me.' The merchant is just enough in his own conceit, if before men he cannot be convicted of theft. The artificer and craftsman thinketh himself free before God, albeit that he neither work sufficient stuff nor yet sell for reasonable price. 'The world is evil,' saith he, 'and how can men live if they do not as others do?' And thus doth every man lean on the iniquity of another, and thinketh himself sufficiently excused when that he meeteth craft with craft, and repulseth back violence either with deceit or else with open injury. Let us be assured, dear brethren, that these be the sins which heretofore have provoked God not only to plague, but also to destroy and utterly overthrow strong realms and flourishing commonwealths." [1]

It was by the lowly pathway of the conviction of sin that Knox, like the other Reformers, reached the position that salvation must come from the mercy of God, and not from his own works; but

[1] *Works*, vi. 413.

there was also another path—a more imperial one—by which, again in common with the other Reformers, he came to the same point. This was the belief in Election. All the Reformers of the sixteenth century were diligent students of Augustine, from whom they learned more than from any other source, with the exception of the Bible. From him they imbibed their faith in the doctrine of predestination. But, indeed, the predestinarian system suits well the exigencies of a time of change and struggle; because it supports the protagonists with a sense that they are the instruments of a divine purpose, and that they are immortal till their work is done. It falls in, besides, with the experience of men who have been awakened to a sense of true religion in a catastrophic manner, as had been the case with the Reformers. Such men are intensely conscious of an immediate divine efficiency in their conversion; they think with amazement of the grace which has made the difference between their former and their present selves; and with equal awe they think of the difference between themselves and the rest of the world. It seems to them that a special act of divine discrimination has lifted them up out of the horrible pit and the miry clay.

To persons theologizing in this mood salvation seems all of God from first to last. He has planned it from eternity; He has worked it out in the incarnation and passion of His Son and in the institution and the ordinances of the Church; and He will see to it that in the receivers also all the experiences shall come to pass which are necessary to ensure that His own redeeming purpose is not in vain. Thus arises a system like Calvinism, in which the sovereign but glorious and loving will of God holds sway from eternity to eternity, and the drama of creation ends in the redemption of a multitude which no man can number. But there is a cooler religious mood in which facts and truths come into prominence of which this fervid theology takes little reckoning. To the latter it matters little what difference there is between man and man; for all are condemned and all may equally be saved; but undoubtedly there are great differences between one sinner and another, and for certain purposes even in religion it is essential to bear this in mind. To a system like Calvinism the difference between one saint and another appears of very minor importance; indeed, the better saint of the two may be the more conscious of his own shortcomings, and in the end both will equally be saved. But, from other points of view, the differences between those who bear respectively thirty, forty and an hundredfold are enormous, and to overlook these is to lose some of the most pathetic motives of morality. In this cooler atmosphere a system like Arminianism has its birth ; and undoubtedly such a system has its own share of truth ; although Calvinism is the purer expression of the religious sentiment at its warmest—when it is lost in God and acknowledges that He must be all in all.

It was on this subject that Knox wrote his longest theological work—*An Answer to the Cavillations of an Adversary respecting the Doctrine of Predestination.* The adversary was the author of a book entitled *Careless by Necessity* ; but no copy of this work has been found, and the author is only doubtfully identified with a certain Robert Cooke, known to have been in those days a disseminator of the opinions here assailed. These included not only anti-Calvinism, but perfectionism, toleration, and the miscellaneous heresies embraced within the comprehensive name of Anabaptism. Knox had known the author at an earlier stage of his career, when he was a person of promise ; and he frequently bewails his backsliding, once going so far as to say that he would be willing to give his own soul for his reclamation. It would appear that he was a person of indifferent learning ; and Knox occasionally talks down to him from the platform of a thoroughly educated man, acquainted with the tongues; but, for all that, he must have been a thinker of no little acuteness; his book had obviously created something of a panic in the circles for whose benefit Knox wrote this refutation; and Knox has sometimes enough to do when attempting to invalidate his arguments.

These he quotes in his antagonist's own words, often at great length, and then subjoins a refutation. This plan gives the book a clumsy appearance, occasioning innumerable repetitions; and the work must be confessed to be more a collection of fragments than a comprehensive or masterly treatment of a great subject. Indeed, at the commencement, the author writes in a singularly helpless manner, as if he were engaged in handling tools which he had not learned how to use. There is an extraordinary contrast between the dulness of this work and the piquancy of *The History of the Reformation*. Obviously the one was written *invitâ Minervâ* and to order, the other straight from the heart. Yet the book improves as it proceeds; and the author naïvely betrays his own consciousness of getting on better; saying, about the middle, " Behold how smoothly God conducteth our tossed boat through the raging waves of your furious arguments "; and, somewhat later, " Behold your spider-webs with less labour dissolved and burst

than, I am assured, you and your great captain
Castellio did spin, knit and weave the same." He
kindles into true warmth and eloquence when
refuting the slander, which has been so often
launched against Calvinism, that it encourages its
adherents to live as they please ; and he anticipates
Froude in repelling this argument by pointing to
the moral condition of the cities or countries
where Calvinism has been embraced. The instance
chosen by him is naturally Geneva ; and here is
his flattering description of that city :—

"What maketh the poor city of Geneva—poor,
I say, in man's eyes, but rich before God, by the
plentiful abundance of His heavenly graces—what
maketh it, I say, so odious to the carnal men of this
world ? Assuredly not this doctrine wherewith ye
charge us ; for that could well please the carnal
man, to let him live at his pleasure without all
punishment. Is it not the right rigour of justice
and the severity of discipline executed therein, in
such sort that no manifest offender, wheresoever he
hath committed his offence, doth there escape
punishment ? Is not this it that so doth offend not
only the licentious of the world, but even you dissembling hypocrites cannot abide that the sword
of God's vengeance shall strike the murderer, the
blasphemer, and such others as God by His Word

commandeth to die ?  Not so by your judgments :
he must live : he may repent.  And those commonwealths do ye highly praise where men may live as
they wish, be subject to no law nor order ; yea,
where the drunkard and such other abominable
persons are permitted to live quietly and find favour
to escape punishment and shame.  But, because in
the streets of Geneva dare no notable malefactor
shew his face (all praise and glory be unto God)
any more than dare the owl in the bright sun,
therefore is it hated." [1]

All the usual arguments against Calvinism are
adduced in the words of the adversary, and then
refuted one by one.  There is much quoting of
Scripture on both sides, with somewhat desperate
shifts occasionally to escape the force of texts
which seem to be hostile, and not infrequently
the use of texts as proofs which stand themselves
in need of explaining.  The contention mainly turns
on the question whether human responsibility is
compatible with divine foreordination ; the adversary
holding that those who perish are not responsible
for being lost, if they were doomed to perish before
their birth, while Knox insists that they perish
justly for their sins ; for he is perfectly clear that
this is the correct statement of the case : " Most

[1] *Works,* v. 211.

unjustly you accuse us, laying to our charge that
we burden God to be the cause of condemnation,
the which we all with one consent impute to man,
to sin, and to the Devil, the first solicitor to sin."
He refuses to be charged with holding that the
greater part of the human race are foredoomed to
perdition, as Calvinists do not profess to know
the numbers of the saved or the lost ; and he re-
jects with holy abhorrence the reproach that God,
according to his teaching, is the author of sin.
Towards the close he carries the war into the
enemy's country by an account of the origin and
tenets of the Anabaptists, and especially of the
vagaries of Peter Münzer and the fanatics of
Münster.

It is curious how in our own day this mysterious
subject should have been brought again to the
front through the decision pronounced in the House
of Lords on 1 August 1904, in the case between
the United Free Church of Scotland and the body
of its former members who did not enter the Union,
the Lord Chancellor declaring the Calvinism of
the Confession of Faith to be irreconcilable with
the free offer of the Gospel, as this is vindicated
in the Declaratory Act of 1892. This is an ob-
jection to Calvinism of similar character with many
brought against it in this book ; but it can scarcely

be said to be specifically dealt with by Knox;
and I am not certain if he would have come
well out of an argument on such a theme; for
the adversary did bring against him such texts
as the one which states that God delighteth not
in the death of the wicked, and the other which
asserts that He will have all men to be saved;
and his manner of dealing with these is not
very satisfactory. He limits and minimises their
significance, instead of glorying in the magnanimity
of God, which they reveal. The truth is, the Church
has learned since Knox's time to welcome more
gladly and to preach more emphatically this side
of Scriptural truth. In the days of Knox there
were no foreign missions, and these have done
much to open the mind and heart of Christendom
to many aspects of divine revelation, and this
one among the rest.

Calvinists believe in election not only because
it is revealed in Scripture, but because it is
confirmed by experience. Every redeemed man
knows that he would never have thought of God
unless God had first thought of him. God can
say to all Christians, "Ye have not chosen Me,
but I have chosen you"; and these answer, in
their turn, "We love Him because He first loved
us." But, on the other hand, even clearer and

*Contra*

ampler is the testimony of Scripture that God is calling all, and that the Saviour is offered to all without distinction. This also is not only revealed by Scripture, but confirmed by experience; because, the more anyone is occupied in seeking and saving the lost, the more sensible does he become of entering into the very mind and heart of God; and, the more the Church carries out the Saviour's command to preach the Gospel to every creature, the more does it know itself to be in harmony with the divine will. There is, it must be confessed, a mystery in this subject which we cannot now penetrate and which may be too deep for the human faculties. But election and the free offer of the Gospel are both manifestations of the one redeeming love of God: they are portions of one shining arc, the curve of which shows that they are destined to meet, although the meeting-point is shrouded in the clouds and thick darkness of Deity.

# CHAPTER III.

## *HIS POLITICAL OPINIONS*

ONLY less important to his native land than his religious views were the Scottish Reformer's political opinions. To himself, in all probability, the two appeared to be one ; and, ever since, in the Scottish mind the waters of religious and political conviction have been in close proximity, with a constant tendency to mingle. Substantially the same political ideas as his were propounded at the same time by George Buchanan in his work, *De Jure Regni apud Scotos*, but the renowned Humanist wrote in a foreign tongue, whereas Knox conveyed his message in the vernacular ; and, while Buchanan addressed himself to the learned few, Knox thundered his opinions into the ears of the multitude with the force and passion of an orator. In the generations which have intervened between his day and our own, his ideas have been working like a leaven in the mind of the Scottish people ; and to him may in no small measure be ascribed the type of political conviction, robust in character yet tinged with reverence, which has been the prevailing one north of the Border.

As early as 1554 we find Knox in correspondence with Bullinger, the Reformer of Zurich, on the following questions, which show how much his mind was occupied with politics : 1. Whether the son of a king, upon his father's death, though unable by reason of his tender age to conduct the government of the kingdom, is nevertheless by right of inheritance to be regarded as a lawful magistrate and as such to be obeyed as of divine right ? 2. Whether a female can preside over and rule a kingdom by divine right, and so transfer the right of sovereignty to her husband ? 3. Whether obedience is to be rendered to a magistrate who enforces idolatry and condemns true religion, and whether those authorities that are still in military occupation of towns and fortresses are permitted to repel this ungodly violence from themselves and their friends ? 4. To which party must godly persons attach themselves in the case of a religious nobility resisting an idolatrous sovereign ?[1] Ten years later, in a committee of the General Assembly, he debated topics of the same kind, at great length and in high spirits, with

[1] *Works*, iii. 221 ff.

Maitland of Lethington, the only man on the opposite side who was able to stand up to him in argument ; and the decision with which he then summed up the debate proved that in the interval he had made up his own mind on nearly every point.[1] The ripening process may be seen going on in such productions of his pen, between these two dates, as his *Appellation to the Nobility* and his *Letter to the Commonalty of Scotland*, issued on the eve of his final return to his native land, and especially in a series of proclamations which he sent out, in the name of the Lords of the Congregation, during the progress of the civil war waged with Mary of Guise.

It cannot be considered a circumstance favourable to Knox's political reputation that his best known contribution to political doctrine is *The First Blast of the Trumpet against the Monstrous Regiment of Women*, in which he maintains the thesis that to allow a woman to occupy a throne is contrary to both reason and Scripture. This treatise was published in the very year when the reign began which it has been usual to consider the most illustrious in British history, and this was the reign

[1] *History*, ii. 425 ff.

of a woman ; and, if we read it now, it is with the memory fresh in our minds of the only other reign in our annals which can compete with that of Elizabeth—the glorious reign of Queen Victoria. Against such a refutation of facts no logic can successfully contend ; and, therefore, it is scarcely worth while to recall the arguments of the author. Suffice it to say, that he unfolded no inconsiderable learning in the quotation of authorities, both classical and Christian, on his side, and that he wielded the argument from Scripture with his usual copiousness and ingenuity. Happily, he had left himself a loophole of escape, by allowing that there might be exceptions to the rule ; but Queen Elizabeth was not likely to be much mollified by his offer to give her the benefit of this doubt, when it was conveyed in the following terms :—

"Nothing in my book contained is or can be prejudicial to your Grace's just regiment, provided that you be not found ungrateful unto God. Ungrate you shall be proved in presence of His throne, howsoever the flatterers justify your acts, if you transfer the glory of that in which you now stand to any other thing than to the dispensation of His mercies, which only maketh that truthful to your Grace which nature and law denieth to all women. Neither would I that

your Grace should fear that this your humilia-
tion before God should, in any case, infirm and
weaken your just and lawful authority before men.
Nay, Madam, such unfeigned confession of God's
benefits received shall be the establishment of the
same, not only to yourself but also to your seed
and posterity ; where, contrariwise, a proud conceit
and elevation of yourself shall be the occasion that
your reign shall be unstable, troublesome and short.
God is witness that unfeignedly I both reverence
and love your Grace ; yea, I pray that your reign
may be long, prosperous and quiet ; and that for
the quietness which Christ's members, before persecuted, have received under you.   Yet, if I should
flatter your Grace, I were no friend, but a deceitful
traitor ; and, therefore, of conscience I am compelled
to say, that neither the consent of people, process
of time, nor multitude of men can establish a law
which God shall approve ; but, whatsoever He ap-
proveth by His eternal Word that shall be approved,
and whatsoever He damneth that shall be condemned, though all men on earth should hazard the
justification of the same.   And therefore, Madam, the
only way to retain and keep these benefits of God,
abundantly poured out of late days upon you and
your realm, is unfeignedly to render unto God's
mercy and undeserved grace the whole glory of this

your exaltation. Forget your birth and all title
which thereupon doth hang, and consider deeply
how for fear of your life you did decline from
God and bow in idolatry. Let it not appear a
small offence in your eyes that you have declined
from Christ Jesus in the day of His battle. Neither
yet would I that you should esteem the mercy
to be vulgar and common which you have received,
to wit, that God hath covered your former offences,
hath preserved you when you were most unthankful,
and in the end hath exalted and raised you up
not only from the dust but also from the ports
of death to rule over His people for the comfort
of His Kirk. It appertaineth to you, therefore, to
ground the justness of your authority not upon
that law which from year to year doth change,
but upon the eternal providence of Him who,
contrary to nature and without your deserving,
hath thus exalted your head. If thus in God's
presence you humble yourself, as in my heart I
glorify God for that rest granted to His afflicted
flock within England under you, a weak instrument,
so will I with tongue and pen justify your authority
and regiment as the Holy Ghost hath justified
the same in Deborah, that blessed mother in Israel.
But, if these premises (as God forbid) be neglected,
and you shall begin to brag of your birth and

build your authority upon your law, flatter you whoso list, your felicity shall be short. Interpret my words in the best part, as written by him who is no enemy to your Grace."

For government in the abstract Knox had the profoundest veneration. He abhorred anarchy, and, when he heard in Geneva that some of the adherents of the Reformation in Scotland were thinking of revolution, he wrote an earnest letter of dissuasion, hinting to them that they were being made the dupes of political adventurers. But government must be good government—that is to say, it must be favourable to the happiness and the virtue of the subjects—this is the assumption lying at the back of all Knox's political theories. He regarded government as a divine arrangement for preserving order in human affairs, and for making it easy to live righteously and difficult to live un-righteously, so that thereby the population should grow up healthy and wealthy, and the resources of the country be developed. For such a govern-ment there is requisite in princes and those who stand beside them at the head of affairs a serious mind, because a great trust is committed to them— the welfare of tens of thousands. They have to be parents and shepherds to the people, and their honour lies in the prosperity and improvement of those over whom they rule.

In our day such ideas are common property, and their justice will be generally admitted. In literature the king is represented to be

> but as the hind
> To whom a space of land is given to plough,
> Who may not wander from the allotted field
> Before his work be done;

and in speculations about the vocation of the states-man he is always viewed as a servant of the public. In short, the maxim of our Lord in the Gospel is penetrating the general mind, that greatness is measured by service. But it requires slight know-ledge of history to be aware how little this has been realised in the past, and especially how little favour it has found in courts. There greatness has generally been measured by a very different standard; the position of a prince being considered an opportunity for indulgence, and even the Decalogue being assumed to be relaxed in his favour. Not the duties of kings, but their prerogatives have been the favourite topics of court philosophers and court preachers. In the century after that of Knox the divine right of kings was the doctrine oftenest heard-of at the court of the Stuarts; and James the First of England was well aware that John Knox had been no friend of the supremacy to which he laid claim.[1]

But what was to happen if government should be bad—if, instead of promoting the welfare of the people, it fastened on their necks a yoke of oppression, and if, instead of promoting religion and virtue, it fostered superstition and encouraged immorality? This was the question which Scotland had to face in the evil days of Mary of Guise, when the country was overrun with French soldiery, and in those of Mary Stuart, when French manners were introduced at court and the attempt was made to overturn the Protestant Reformation; and Scotland looked for the answer to John Knox.

To him it was axiomatic that there must be some remedy. It never occurred to him that a country should put up with bad government on account of the supposed rights of princes. To his mind the supreme right was that of the country to enjoy good order and to advance in the path of progress.

First, in such an event he would have recourse to the nobility, who, he maintained, held their places and honours for no other end than the benefit of the citizens in general. "My petition," says he, "is, that ye, whom God hath appointed heads in your

---

[1] See a remarkable utterance of his quoted by Laing in *Works*, iv. 435.

commonwealth, with single eye do study to promote the glory of God ; to provide that your subjects be rightly instructed in His true religion ; that they may be defended from all oppression and tyranny ; that true teachers may be maintained and such as blind and deceive the people, together with all idle bellies, which do rob and oppress the flock, may be removed and punished as God's law prescribeth. And to the performance of every one of these do your offices and names, the honours and benefits which ye receive, the law of God universally given to all men, and the examples of most godly princes bind and oblige you." " Be not deceived, my Lords," he adds, " ye are placed in authority for another purpose than to flatter your king in his folly and blind rage : to wit, that, as with your strength, riches and wisdom ye are bound to assist and defend him in all things which by your advice he shall take in hand for God's glory, so by your gravities, counsel and admonition ye are bound to correct and repress whatsoever ye know him to attempt expressly repugning to God's Word, honour and glory, or what ye shall espy him to do, be it by ignorance or be it by malice, against his subjects great or small." [1]

But, if nobles as well as kings should turn out to be impracticable, there was still a resource in

[1] *Works*, iv. 480, 493.

the people themselves; and to this body Knox did not hesitate to appeal in these terms: " Although ye be but subjects, ye may lawfully require of your superiors, be it of your king, be it of your lords, rulers and powers, that they provide for you true preachers, and that they expel such as, under the name of pastors, devour and destroy the flock, not feeding the same as Christ Jesus has commanded. And, if in this point your superiors be negligent, or yet pretend to maintain tyrants in their tyranny, most justly ye may provide true teachers for yourselves, be it in your cities, towns or villages. Them ye shall maintain and defend against all that shall persecute them and by that means shall labour to defraud you of that most comfortable food of your souls, Christ's Evangel truly preached. Ye may, moreover, withhold the fruits and profits which your false bishops and clergy most unjustly receive of you, until such time as they be compelled faithfully to do their charge and duties, which is to preach unto you Christ Jesus truly, rightly to minister the sacraments according to His own institution, and so to watch for the salvation of your souls."

In such words there are surely the seeds of things which, since then, have grown in Scotland and the world, although they have not even yet come to full maturity; as, indeed, in the *Letter to the*

*Commonalty of Scotland*, in which they occur, the author rises to the highest pitch of eloquence of which he is capable: " Neither would I," says he, " that you should esteem the reformation and care of religion less to appertain to you, because you are no kings, judges, rulers, nobles, nor in authority. Beloved brethren, you are God's creatures, created and formed in His own image and similitude, for whose redemption was shed the most precious blood of the only beloved Son of God, to whom He hath commanded His Gospel and glad tidings to be preached, and for whom He hath prepared the heavenly inheritance, so that you will not obstinately refuse and disdainfully condemn the means which He hath appointed to obtain the same : to wit, His blessed Evangel, which He now offereth to you to the end that you may be saved. For the Gospel and glad tidings of the kingdom truly preached is the power of God to the salvation of every believer, which to credit and receive you, the commonalty, are no less bound than are your rulers and princes. For, albeit God hath put and ordained distinction and difference betwixt the king and subjects, betwixt the rulers and the common people, in the regiment and the administration of civil policies, yet in the hope of the life to come He hath made all equal. For as in Christ Jesus the Jew hath no greater prerogative than has the Gentile, the man than hath the woman, the learned than the unlearned, the lord than the servant, but all are one in Him, so is there but one way and means to attain to the participation of His benefits and spiritual graces, which is a lively faith working by charity. And, therefore, I say, that it doth no less appertain to you, beloved brethren, to be assured that your faith and religion be grounded and established upon the true and undoubted Word of God than to your princes or rulers."[1]

The constitutional idea embodied in the title of the treatise of Samuel Rutherford on Government, which is one of the landmarks in the history of politics—*Lex Rex*—was not unknown in the days of Knox. At the meeting of the committee of the General Assembly already mentioned, it was propounded by John Craig, the colleague of Knox in Edinburgh, who said that, when attending the University of Bologna, he had heard it stated in a disputation in these terms—" that all rulers, be they supreme or be they inferior, may and ought to be reformed and deposed by them by whom they are chosen, confirmed or admitted to their office, as oft as they break that promise made by oath to their subjects; because that their prince is no

[1] *Works*, iv. 534, 526.

less bound by oath to the subjects than are the subjects to their princes ; and, therefore, ought they to be kept and reformed equally, according to the law and condition of the oath that is made of either party " ; and to this doctrine Craig signified his own adherence. In Knox's mind regal authority was not based on a contract like this, assumed to subsist between rulers and subjects and liable to be dissolved in case the ruler proved untrue to it, but rather on a pledge assumed to be given by the prince to God, who withdraws His support, when the pledge is broken, and so lets the throne topple to the ground. By committing capital crimes—and it has to be remembered that in Knox's estimation adultery and idolatry are to be numbered among these, and that in his eyes the Mass was idolatry— a king or queen was, just as much as a private person, rendered liable to capital punishment ; and, in places where such crimes are perpetrated by princes, it is not only lawful to punish to the death those who are guilty of them, " but the magistrates and people are bound so to do, unless they will provoke the wrath of God against themselves." " And, therefore," he adds, " I fear not to affirm that it had been the duty of the nobility, judges, rulers and people of England, not only to have resisted and gainstanded Mary, that Jezebel, whom they call their Queen, but also to have punished her to the death, with all the sort of her idolatrous priests, together with all such as should have assisted her, what time that she and they openly began to suppress Christ's Evangel, to shed the blood of the saints of God, and to erect that most devilish idolatry, the Pope's abominations, and his usurped tyranny, that once most justly by common oath was banished from that realm."[1]    And the same principles are explicitly stated in the following programme of what was to be *The Second Blast of the Trumpet* :—

" 1. It is not birth only, nor propinquity of blood, that maketh a king lawfully to reign above a people professing Christ Jesus and His eternal verity; but in his election must the ordinance, which God hath established in the election of inferior judges, be observed ; 2. No manifest idolater nor notorious transgressor of God's holy precepts ought to be promoted to any public regiment, honour or dignity in any realm, province or city that hath subjected themselves to Christ Jesus and to His blessed Evangel ; 3. Neither can oath nor promise bind any such people to obey and maintain tyrants against God, and against His truth known ; 4. But, if either rashly they have promoted any manifest wicked person or yet ignorantly have chosen such

[1] *Works*, iv. 509.

an one as after declareth himself unworthy of regiment above the people of God (and such be all idolaters and cruel persecutors), most justly may the same men depose and punish him that unadvisedly before they did nominate, appoint and elect." [1]

Not only did Knox hold these principles in theory, but he put them into practice. When he arrived in Scotland in 1559, he found the country, as we have seen, enveloped in the flames of civil war, and he did not hesitate to plunge into the revolution. On him fell the responsibility of justifying the procedure of those with whom he had identified himself; and, from the camp of the rebels, he issued manifesto after manifesto, expounding the situation to his fellow-countrymen and endeavouring to secure their co-operation in the struggle. The most vivid and condensed, however, of these productions of his pen at this crisis is one which does not appear to have been published with the authority of the Lords of the Congregation, perhaps because it was too strong even for their taste; but it is a document essential to those who wish to behold the very Knox as he really was; and, therefore, it shall be given in full :—

"If it be seditious to speak the truth in all sobriety, and to complain when they are wounded,

[1] *Works*, iv. 537.

or to call for help against unjust tyranny before
that their throats be cut, then can we not deny
but we are criminal and guilty of tumult and
sedition. For we have said that our commonwealth is oppressed, that we and our brethren are
hurt by the tyranny of strangers, and that we fear
bondage and slavery, seeing that multitudes of
cruel murderers are daily brought in our country
without our counsel, or knowledge and consent.
We dispute not so much whether the bringing in
of more Frenchmen be violating of the Appointment
(which the Queen nor her faction cannot deny
to be manifestly broken by them, in more cases
than one) as that we would know, if the heaping
of strangers upon strangers above us, without our
counsel or consent, be a thing that may stand
with the liberty of our realm and with the profit
of our commonwealth. It is not unknown to all
men of judgment, that the fruits of our country
in the most common years are no more than
sufficiently reasonable to nourish the born inhabitants
of the same. But now, seeing that we have been
vexed with wars, taken upon us at the pleasure
of France, by which the most fruitful portion of
our country in corn has been wasted ; what man
is so blind but that he may see, that such bands
of ungodly and idle soldiers can be nothing else

but an occasion to famish our poor brethren ? And in this point we refuse not (which is the chief) the judgment of all natural Scottish men.

"The Queen Regent alleged 'that although there were a hundred Frenchmen for one in Scotland, yet she is not minded to trouble any in his just possession.' Whereto we answer, that we dispute not what she intends (which, nevertheless, by probable conjectures, is to be suspected) but always we affirm, that such a multitude of Frenchmen is a burden, not only unprofitable but also intolerable to this poor realm ; for the poor commons of this realm have sustained them with the sweat of their brows, since the contracting of the peace and somewhat before. What motherly affection she has declared to this realm and to the inhabitants of the same, her works have evidently declared ever since the first hour that she has borne authority ; and, albeit men will not this day see what danger hangs over their heads, yet fear we, that ere it be long, experience shall teach some that we fear not without cause. The cruel murder and oppression used by them whom now she fosters is to us a sufficient argument, what is to be looked for, when her number is so multiplied that our force shall not be able to gainstand their tyranny.

"Where she complains of our preachers, affirming

that irreverently they speak of princes in general and of her in particular, inducing the people thereby to defection from their duty, etc., and, therefore, that such a thing cannot be suffered, because this occasion is had against God's true ministers, we cannot but witness what tread and order of doctrine they have kept, and yet keep on that point. In public prayers they commend to God all princes in general and the magistrates of this our native realm in particular. In open audience they declare the authority of princes and magistrates to be of God ; and therefore they affirm that they ought to be honoured, feared, obeyed, even for conscience' sake ; provided that they command nor require nothing expressly repugning to God's commandment and plain will, revealed in His holy Word. Moreover, they affirm that, if wicked persons, abusing the authority established by God, command things manifestly wicked, that such as may and do bridle the inordinate appetites of princes cannot be accused as resisters of the authority which is God's good ordinance. To bridle the fury and rage of princes in free kingdoms and realms, they affirm it appertains to the nobility, sworn and born counsellors of the same, and also to the barons and people, whose votes and consent are to be required in all great and weighty matters of the commonwealth.

Which if they do not, they declare themselves criminal with their princes, and so subject to the same vengeance of God, which they deserve for that they pollute the seat of justice and do, as it were, make God author of iniquity. They proclaim and they cry, that the same God who plagued Pharaoh, repulsed Sennacherib, struck Herod with worms, and made the bellies of dogs the grave and sepulchre of despiteful Jezebel, will not spare the cruel princes, murderers of Christ's members in this our time. In this manner they speak of princes in general and of your Grace in particular.

" This only we have heard one of our preachers say, rebuking the vain excuse of such as flatter themselves, by reason of the authority : ' Many now-a-days,' said he, ' will have no other religion or faith than the Queen and the authority had.' But is it not possible, that the Queen be so far blinded that she will have no religion, nor no other faith, than may content the Cardinal of Lorraine ? And may it not likewise be that the Cardinal be so corrupt that he will admit no religion which does not establish the Pope in his kingdom ? But plain it is that the Pope is lieutenant to Satan and enemy to Christ Jesus and to His perfect religion. Let men, therefore, consider what danger they stand in, if their salvation shall depend upon the Queen's faith and religion. Further we have never heard any of our preachers speak of the Queen Regent, neither publicly nor privately.

"Where her Grace declares it will not be suffered that our preachers meddle with policy, nor speak of her nor of other princes but with reverence, we answer that, as we will justify and defend nothing in our preachers which we find not God to have justified and allowed in His messengers before them, so dare we not forbid them openly to reprehend that which the Spirit of God, speaking in the prophets and apostles, has reprehended before them. Elijah did personally reprove Ahab and Jezebel of idolatry, of avarice, of murder ; and, such like, Isaiah the prophet called the magistrates of Jerusalem in his times companions to thieves, princes of Sodom, bribe-takers and murderers. He complained that their silver was turned into dross, that their wine was mingled with water, and that justice was bought and sold. Jeremiah said that the bones of king Jehoiakim should wither with the sun. Christ Jesus called Herod a fox, and Paul called the High Priest a painted wall, and prayed unto God that He should strike him, because that against justice he commanded him to be smitten. Now, if the like or greater corruptions be in the world this day, who dare enterprise to put silence to the Spirit of God, which will not be subject to the appetites of wicked princes ? " [1]

It cannot be denied that the continual agitation of such fundamental questions would be dangerous to the tranquillity of any state. But the apology of Knox would be, that his was an exceptional time, and that the thorough discussion of the principles applicable to such a period of transition tended to prevent the recurrence of the evils against which extreme measures had to be taken.

To the rights of bad rulers Knox turned an ear as deaf as that of the adder ; but, it being assumed that a ruler of the right stamp had been secured, he would have entrusted him with very comprehensive powers indeed. Even to Mary of Lorraine, at a time when he still had hope of winning her to the Protestant side, he suffered himself to say : " You think, peradventure, that the care of religion is not committed to magistrates, but to the bishops and estate ecclesiastical, as they term it. No, no, the negligence of bishops shall no less be required of the hands of magistrates, because they foster and maintain them in tyranny, than shall the oppression of false judges, whom kings maintain and defend." [2] And, in a similar

[1] *History*, i. 409.  [2] *Works*, iv. 69.

strain, he says to the Scottish nobility in the Appellation already quoted : " I am not ignorant that Satan of old time, for maintenance of his darkness, hath obtained of the blind world two chief points—former, he hath persuaded princes, rulers and magistrates that the feeding of Christ's flock appertaineth nothing to their charge, but that it is devolved upon the bishops and estate ecclesiastical ; and, secondarily, that the reformation of religion, be it ever so corrupt, and the punishment of such as be sworn soldiers in their kingdom, are exempted from all civil power and are reserved to themselves and to their own cognition. But that no offender can be justly exempted from punishment, and that the ordering and reformation of religion with the instruction of subjects doth especially appertain to the civil magistrate, shall God's perfect ordinance, His plain Word, and the facts and examples of those that of God are highly praised, most evidently declare."

So far was he prepared to go, on the assumption that the ruler was of the right character and on his own side, that he sanctioned persecution and spoke of toleration with scorn. Writing from Geneva, he does not scruple to associate himself with those who burnt Servetus, even saying that that heretic's opinions deserved ten thousand deaths. He was not without warning ; for the acute anta-

gonist against whom he wrote his treatise on Predestination had shrewdly remarked of the Calvinists :
" They put forth books, affirming it to be lawful
to persecute and put to death such as dissent from
them in controversies of religion, whom they call
blasphemers of God. Notwithstanding they, afore
they came to authority, were of another judgment,
and did both say and write, that no man ought
to be persecuted for conscience' sake. Yet now they
are not only become persecutors, but also they have
given, as far as lieth in them, the sword into the
hands of bloody tyrants." [1]

It is indeed surprising that the mind of Knox
did not perceive this to be, in fact, the logical issue
of his principles. But his eyes were holden. For
such a man as he, it is not enough to plead
that intolerance was the doctrine of the age, and
even of generations after him ; because he ought
to have risen above his age. It would, indeed,
be unfair to blame him for not being able to
determine with accuracy at all points the relation
of Church and state ; for this involves problems
which have demanded the thought and experience
of centuries, and are not perfectly solved yet ; but
by his own sufferings and those of his friends he ought
to have been better instructed on the subject of

[1] *Works*, v. 208.

religious persecution ; and it is a blot on his political memory that he did not judge more charitably. Still more must it be reckoned to him for unrighteousness, as an ecclesiastical statesman, that he approved of the barbarous actions by which the country got rid of Cardinal Beaton and David Rizzio.

# BOOK THIRD

## HIS IDEALS

# CHAPTER I.

## THE SCOTS CONFESSION OF FAITH

I T has already been remarked that, in his life-time, John Knox was credited with being a prophet; and there is nothing which more tends to attract to anyone the curiosity and veneration of other human beings than the impression that he is able to lift a corner of the curtain of futurity. Perhaps he was not himself altogether averse to the interest in his person excited by this vague belief; but, on the whole, his views on the subject were perfectly sane: "My assurances," he said, "are not the marvels of Merlin nor yet the dark sentences of profane prophecies. But, first, the plain truth of God's Word, secondly, the invincible justice of the everlasting God, and, thirdly, the ordinary course of His punishments and plagues are my assurance and grounds. God's Word threateneth destruction to all inobedient; His immutable justice must require the same; the ordinary punishments and plagues show examples. What man, then, can cease to prophesy? "[1]   To prophecy of this sort it is evident that anyone may attain in his degree who observes the course of events with a watchful eye and, at the same time, familiarises himself with the principles of Providence, as these are revealed in the Holy Scriptures.   But it is in a more modern sense that we now speak of Knox as a prophet, as Carlyle has done in his remarkable estimate of his fellow-countryman in *Heroes and Hero-Worship*. By a prophet we mean one who has had a vision of what his country might become by advancing along a certain pathway, and who has with eloquence and effect pointed this pathway out.   In this sense Knox holds a conspicuous place among modern prophets ; for it is certain that he yearned over his native country with an intense affection, saw with unrivalled clearness what were the conditions of its true welfare, and impressed these in memorable words on the mind of Scotland.

When in those days a man of prophetic character thus saw a vision of the future, it was apt to assume the form of a structure of which the foundation was a Confession of Faith, the walls a Book of Discipline, and the roof or pinnacle a Book of

[1] *Works*, iii. 168.

Common Order. These were the products to which, at the epoch of the Reformation, the efforts of the foremost minds were directed ; and we have now to see how far Knox succeeded in shaping them for the use of his country.

Confessions of faith were peculiar products of the Reformation era. In the Early Church, indeed, immense labour had been expended on a few brief documents of the same order, the best known of which are the Apostles' Creed and the Nicene Creed ; but the activity of the Church in this direction had ceased for a thousand years when, at the Reformation, it was resumed again ; and now the creeds proved to be of much greater extent. Every country in which the work of reformation made any considerable progress had its own ; but the most renowned were the German, entitled the Augsburg Confession, the Swiss, called the First Helvetic Confession, and the Articles of the Church of England.

The primary object of them all was to make known the new revelation of the truth of God which had visited men's souls, the recently discovered art of printing being made available for the purpose of diffusing the message with which the minds of those who issued the confessions were charged. Creeds had originally arisen out of the practice of permitting converts to bear witness at their baptism, in the presence of the onlookers, to the faith they had embraced, the Apostles' Creed being nothing else than the formula in which this was done. In the earliest times, there is reason to believe, this was regarded as a privilege and an honour by those who thus testified to the world what the Saviour had done for them. Certainly at the Reformation it was a strong religious impulse that inspired the composition of confessions : they were the spontaneous and irresistible expression of strong convictions. And obviously this ought to be a characteristic of such documents always, or they have ceased to deserve their name. If a Church is not proud of its confession, but only endures it, it is manifest that the salt has lost its savour.

Another object aimed at was the contradiction of false doctrine. It may be due to the inherent laziness of the human mind, which never does hard work till it is compelled ; but it is an acknowledged fact that the Church has never taken a firm grasp of truth except when forced to do so by the emergence of error. All the creeds bear marks of this, for they abound in refutations of doctrines believed to be false ; and against this foil the outline of the truth is made distinct. At the Reformation there was a huge accumulation of error to be got rid of, and the confessions of faith attacked it with energy. In all of them the strongest possible language is applied to the Pope and all his works ; and the way of salvation by free grace is illustrated by contrast with the ceremonies and legalism of the old system. We may shrink now from the epithets employed against opponents and, indeed, from the argumentative and truculent tone in which it was customary at that time to write ; but it is short-sighted not to perceive that this was to a large extent only a fashion of the age, or to miss the exquisite flower concealed within the hard and prickly sheath of controversy.

The most questionable aspect of creeds is their application as tests. Not only at the time were they used to separate the sheep from the goats, but they have been handed down from age to age, often being made a condition of the holding even of secular positions and always of the holding of sacred offices. This is defended, at least for positions of the latter sort, on the ground that the Scripture itself is not a sufficient test, as its words can be assented to by those holding radically opposite opinions. It is argued that to give a

Church compactness there must be an absolutely
definite ground on which all the members stand.
Money will not be given for the propagation of
a Church's tenets, unless the donors have a sufficient
guarantee for the teaching of what they believe to
be the truth. These reasons may be sufficient;
but there are certainly serious items on the opposite
side of the account. When thus employed, creeds
perpetuate the differences between denominations,
whereas these ought to learn from one another
and thus gradually approximate to one another's
standpoints. If they make truth permanent, they
make error permanent also ; as may be seen in
the case of the Church of Rome, which, provoked
by the activity of the Protestants in creed-con-
struction, gave to its own doctrines a confessional
form at the Council of Trent which has cut off
its return to the simplicity of the Gospel. By
all Protestants it is acknowledged that the Bible
is the supreme standard, but there is a constant
temptation to read the Scriptures by the light of
the creed, instead of *vice versa*. It is allowed that
the creed is fallible and that it ought to be changed,
if the Spirit of God, by means of the new light
of Providence, expands and purifies the Church's
apprehensions of the truth ; but, in point of fact,
such an acknowledgment is usually a mere formality,

no alteration actually taking place, and the creed being virtually accorded the same immutability as the Scriptures. In our own day a new terror has been added to life by the discovery that churches may, through their confessions of faith, be dragged into courts of law, where the most sacred elements of doctrine are handled, as if they were coal and tallow, by judges whose acquaintance with the history and contents of the confession has been extemporised and may be neither accurate nor sympathetic. Actual revision, at intervals not too far apart, alone can justify the use of creeds as tests at all.[1]

As has been already indicated, it was in 1560 that the First Scots Confession was drawn up, at the request of Parliament, by Knox and five other divines, all of whom, like himself, bore the name of John—Wynram, Spottiswood, Willock, Douglas and Row. The time in which they completed their task—four days—seems miraculously brief when compared with that required in our day to effect the slightest revision of any creed; but it is not to be forgotten that Knox at any rate was a practised hand. He had co-operated in drawing up the Articles of the Church of England; in Geneva he

[1] Cf. RAINY, *The Delivery and Development of Doctrine*, ch. vi.

had made a rapid sketch of a creed for insertion
in the Prayer Book of the English congregation ;
and he was doubtless familiar with the other confessions already adopted by the Protestant Churches
of the Continent.    But, besides, the composition of
such manifestoes was a favourite occupation of the
age ; and the matter of which they were composed
was common property.

Still the work, which bears very manifestly the
stamp of the genius of its principal author, is a
thoroughly original composition, characterized in
a high degree by the spirit of conviction and en-
thusiasm, which must always be reckoned the
principal virtue of such productions.    Thus, its
opening words are : " Long have we thirsted, dear
brethren, to have notified unto the world the sum
of that doctrine which we profess, and for the which
we have sustained infamy and danger." This is
the true tone of the confessor.    And it was received
in a similar spirit by the Parliament which adopted
it ; great joy being expressed at the birth of such
a testimony, which, it was confidently believed,
would prove a blessing to the nation.

The style is polemical ; not only the Papists being
dealt with in Knox's trenchant manner, but Anabaptists and other contemporary troublers of Israel
being roughly handled, and even ancient heretics,

like Arius, Marcion and Nestorius, receiving a wipe in the bygoing. But the two outstanding features are the exaltation of the Spirit of God above the authority of Fathers and Councils and the exaltation of Christ above the means of grace. The individual is summoned to hear himself the voice of God in the Word, instead of waiting for the reports of those who allege that they have heard it. This responsibility of private judgment lifted the Protestant nations to a new level of manhood; but its truly religious character is never to be overlooked: it is not that the individual is egged-on to place his own opinions above all authority; but he is encouraged to listen in humility to the promptings of the Spirit of God in the way of His own appointment. In like manner it is assumed that there is for the individual direct access to God through Christ; the notion that this can be mediated only through the priest or the Church or the means of grace being alien to this period of religious intuition. Perhaps, indeed, means are placed too much in the background; but, if so, the Confession errs on virtue's side; for means of grace had been put in Christ's place; and they always tend to become obstructions instead of helps.

Knox would not have scrupled to impose the Confession as a test on his own generation; but he does not bear the responsibility of binding it on subsequent ones. On the contrary, he set a flaming example of loyalty to conscience in rejecting the formulas of his predecessors, when these did not agree with the present teachings of the Spirit of God, and, in the Confession itself, occur the following remarkable words, which deserve to be written in letters of gold: "If any man shall note in this our confession any article or sentence repugning to God's Holy Word, may it please him of his gentleness, and for Christian charity's sake, to admonish us of the same in writing; and we of our honour and fidelity do promise unto him satisfaction from the mouth of God (that is, from His Holy Scriptures), or else reformation of that which he shall prove to be amiss."[1]

In point of fact, this First Scots Confession was superseded by the Westminster Confession, after it had existed for less than a hundred years— a period which may be regarded as about the right length of life for such a document. Some, like Edward Irving, have been inclined to consider it superior to that by which it was displaced; but with this I can by no means agree. Knox's production is, indeed, characterized by a verve and a swing which the Westminster Confession lacks; but

[1] *History*, ii. 96.

the latter is far superior as a learned, comprehensive and well-balanced statement.

If asked, however, to produce a specimen of what the Reformation Age in Scotland could do in the way of doctrinal statement, I should select, not any passage of the Confession of Faith, but the following brief creed, found in the Book of Common Order—the subject of the next chapter—and used in administering the ordinance of baptism ; although it must be admitted that it may not be from Knox's own pen ; and, if my instinct is not mistaken, it reads too smoothly to be his in the strictest sense. But at least he sanctioned and used it ; and it may stand as a certificate of his theological competency :—

" The Christian faith, whereof now ye have briefly heard the sum, is commonly divided into twelve articles ; but, that we may the better understand what is contained in the same, we shall divide it into four principal parts. The first shall concern God the Father, the second Jesus Christ our Lord, the third shall express to us our faith in the Holy Ghost, and the fourth and last shall declare what is our faith concerning the Church, and of the graces of God freely given to the same.

" First, of God we confess three things, to wit,

that he is our Father, Almighty, Maker of heaven and earth.

"Our Father we call Him, and so by faith believe Him to be, not so much because He hath created us (for that we have common with the rest of creatures, who yet are not called to that honour to have God to them a favourable Father); but we call Him Father by reason of His free adoption, by the which He hath chosen us to life everlasting in Jesus Christ. And this His most singular mercy we prefer to all things earthly and transitory; for without this there is to mankind no felicity, no comfort nor final joy; and, having this, we are assured that by the same love by the which He once hath freely chosen us He shall conduct the whole course of our life, that in the end we shall possess that immortal kingdom that He hath prepared for His chosen children. For from this fountain of God's free mercy or adoption springeth our vocation, our justification, our continual sanctification, and finally our glorification, as witness the Apostles.

"The same God our Father we confess Almighty, not only in respect of that He may do, but in consideration that by His power and godly wisdom are all creatures in heaven and earth and under the earth ruled, guided and kept in that order

that His eternal will and knowledge hath appointed
them.

"And that is it which in the third part we
do confess, that He is Creator of heaven and earth :
that is to say, that the heaven and the earth,
and the contents thereof, are so in His hand
that there is nothing done without His knowledge
neither yet against His will, but that He ruleth
them so that in the end His godly name shall be
glorified in them.  And so we confess and believe,
that neither the devils nor yet the wicked of the
world have any power to molest or trouble the
chosen children of God but in so far as it pleaseth
Him to use them as instruments, either to prove
and try our faith and patience or else to stir
us to more fervent invocation of His name and
to continual meditation of that heavenly rest and
joy that abideth us after these transitory troubles.
And yet shall not this excuse the wicked, because
they never look in their iniquity to please God
nor yet to obey His will.

"In Jesus Christ we confess two distinct and
perfect natures—to wit, the eternal Godhead and
the perfect Manhood joined together—so that we
confess and believe, that that eternal Word, which
was from the beginning and by the which all things
were created, and yet are conserved and kept in their

being, did, at the time appointed in the counsel of His heavenly Father, receive our nature of a Virgin, by operation of the Holy Ghost. So that in His conception we acknowledge and believe that there is nothing but purity and sanctification; yea, even insomuch as He is become our brother. For it behoved Him that should purge others from their sins to be pure and clean from all spot of sin even from His conception. And, as we confess and believe Him conceived by the Holy Ghost, so do we confess and believe Him to be born of a Virgin named Mary, of the tribe of Judah and of the family of David, that the promise of God and the prophecy might be fulfilled, to wit, 'That the seed of the woman should break down the Serpent's head,' and that 'a Virgin should conceive and bear a child, whose name should be Emmanuel, that is, God with us.' The name Jesus, which signifieth a Saviour, was given unto Him by the Angel, to assure us that it is He alone that saveth His people from their sins. He is called Christ, that is to say, Anointed, by reason of the offices given unto Him by God His Father, to wit, that He alone is appointed King, Priest and Prophet. King, in that all power is given to Him in heaven and earth; so that there is none other but He in heaven nor earth that hath just

authority and power to make laws to bind the
consciences of men ; neither yet is there any other
that may defend our souls from the bondage of
sin, nor yet our bodies from the tyranny of man.
And this He doeth by the power of His Word,
by the which he draweth us out of the bondage
and slavery of Satan and maketh us to reign
over sin ; whilst that we live and serve our God
in righteousness and holiness of our life.  A Priest,
and that perpetual and everlasting, we confess
Him, by reason that by the sacrifice of His own
body, which He once offered up upon the cross,
He hath fully satisfied the justice of his Father
in our behalf ; so that whosoever seeketh any
means besides His death and passion, in heaven
or in earth, to reconcile unto them God's favour,
they do not only blaspheme but also, so far as in
them is, renounce the fruit and efficacy of that
His only one sacrifice.  We confess Him to be
the only Prophet, who hath revealed unto us the
whole will of His Father in all things pertaining
to our salvation.

" This our Lord Jesus we confess to be the only
Son of God, because there is none such by nature
but He alone.  We confess Him also our Lord,
not only by reason we are His creatures but
chiefly because He hath redeemed us by His

precious blood, and so hath gotten just dominion over us, as over the people whom He hath delivered from bondage of sin, death, hell and the Devil, and hath made us kings and priests to God His Father.

" We further confess and believe, that the same our Lord Jesus was accused before an earthly judge, Pontius Pilate, under whom, albeit oft and divers times He was pronounced to be innocent, He suffered the death of the cross, hanged upon a tree betwixt two thieves ; which death, as it was most cruel and vile before the eyes of men, so was it accursed by the mouth of God Himself, saying, ' Cursed is everyone that hangeth on a tree.' And this kind of death sustained He in our person, because He was appointed of God His Father to be our pledge and He that should bear the punishment of our transgressions. And so we acknowledge and believe that He hath taken away that curse and malediction that hanged on us by reason of our sin. He verily died, rendering up His spirit into the hands of His Father, after that He had said, ' Father, into Thy hands I commend my spirit.' After His death, we confess, His body was buried, and that He descended into hell. But, because he was the Author of life, yea, the very Life itself, it was impossible that He should be retained under the dolours of death ; and, therefore,

the third day He rose again victor and conqueror
of death and hell ; by the which His resurrection
He hath brought life again into the world, which
He, by the power of His Holy Spirit, communicateth
unto His lively members ; so that now unto them
corporal death is no death, but an entrance into that
blessed life wherein our Head, Jesus Christ, is now
entered. For, after that He had sufficiently proved
His resurrection to His disciples and unto such
as did constantly abide with Him to the death, He
visibly ascended to the heavens, and was taken from
the eyes of men and placed at the right hand of
God the Father Almighty, where presently He
remaineth in His glory, only Head, only Mediator,
and only Advocate for all the members of His
body ; of which we have most especial comfort ;
first, for that by His ascension the heavens are
opened unto us and an entrance made unto us, that
boldly we may appear before the throne of our
Father's mercy ; and, secondarily, that we know
that this honour and authority is given unto Jesus
Christ, our Head, in our name and for our profit
and utility. For, albeit that in body He now be
in the heaven, yet by the power of His Spirit He
is present here with us, as well to instruct us as
to comfort and maintain us in all our troubles and
adversities, from the which He shall finally deliver

14

His whole Church, and every true member of the same, in that day when He shall visibly appear again, Judge of the quick and the dead.

"For this, finally, we confess of our Lord Jesus Christ, that, as He was seen visibly to ascend, and so left the world, as touching that body that suffered and rose again, so do we constantly believe that He shall come from the right hand of His Father, when all eyes shall see Him, yea, even those that have pierced Him ; and then shall be gathered as well those that then shall be found alive as those that before have slept. Separation shall be made betwixt the lambs and the goats : that is to say, betwixt the elect and the reprobate. The one shall hear this joyful voice, ' Come ye, the blessed of My Father, possess the kingdom that is prepared for you before the beginning of the world.' The other shall hear that fearful and irrevocable sentence, ' Depart from Me, ye workers of iniquity, to the fire that never shall be quenched.' And, for this cause, this day in the Scriptures is called ' the day of refreshing ' and ' of the revelation of all secrets,' because that then the just shall be delivered from all miseries and be possessed in the fulness of their glory. Contrariwise, the reprobate shall receive judgment and recompence of all their impiety, be it openly or secretly wrought.

" As we constantly believe in God the Father and in Jesus Christ, as before is said, so do we assuredly believe in the Holy Ghost, whom we confess God, equal with the Father and the Son, by whose working and mighty operation our darkness is removed, our eyes spiritual are illuminated, our souls and consciences sprinkled with the blood of Jesus Christ, and we retained in the truth of God, even to our lives' end. And, for these causes, we understand that this Eternal Spirit, proceeding from the Father and the Son, hath in the Scriptures divers names. Sometimes is He called water, by reason of His purgation, and giving strength to this our corrupt nature to bring forth good fruit; without whom this our nature should utterly be barren, yea, it should utterly abound in all wickedness. Sometimes the same Spirit is called fire, by reason of the illumination and burning heat of fire that He kindleth in our hearts. The same Spirit also is called oil, or unction, by reason that His working mollifieth the hardness of our hearts and maketh us receive the print of that image of Jesus Christ, by whom only we are sanctified.

" We constantly believe, that there is, was and shall be, even to the coming of the Lord Jesus, a Church, which is holy and universal ; to wit, the Communion of Saints. This Church is holy, because it receiveth

free remission of sins, and that by faith only in
the blood of Jesus Christ. Secondly, because, it
being regenerate, it receiveth the spirit of sanctification and power to walk in newness of life and in
good works, which God hath prepared for His chosen
to walk in. Not that we think the justice of this
Church, or of any member of the same, ever was,
is, or yet shall be, so full and perfect that it needeth
not to stoop under mercy; but, because the imperfections are pardoned and the justice of Jesus
Christ imputed unto such as by true faith cleave
unto Him. Which Church we call universal, because
it consisteth and standeth of all tongues and nations;
yea, of all estates and conditions of men and
women whom of His mercy God calleth from darkness to light and from the bondage and thraldom
of sin to His spiritual service and purity of life.
Unto whom also He communicateth His Holy Spirit,
giving unto them one faith, one head and sovereign
Lord, the Lord Jesus, one Baptism and right use
of Sacraments; whose hearts also He kindleth
together in love and Christian concord.

" To this Church, holy and universal, we acknowledge and believe notable gifts to be granted, to
wit, remission of sins, which by true faith must
be obtained in this life, resurrection of the flesh,
which all shall have, albeit not in equal condition,

for the reprobate (as before is said) shall rise but to fearful judgment and condemnation, and the just shall rise to be possessed in glory. And this resurrection shall not be an imagination, or that one body shall rise for another ; but every man shall receive in his own body as he hath deserved, be it good or evil. The just shall receive the life everlasting, which is the free gift of God given and purchased to His chosen by Jesus Christ, our only Head and Mediator, to whom with the Father and the Holy Ghost, be all honour and glory, now and ever. " [1]

[1] *Works*, vi. 317.

# CHAPTER II.

## THE BOOK OF COMMON ORDER

THE prominence given by Knox and the Scottish Parliament to the Confession of Faith is an eloquent testimony to their belief in truth as the force to change into its own image the character of a nation. Perhaps, indeed, their confidence that pure truth will, as a matter of course, produce pure lives was too sanguine ; because the history of Scotland may be quoted to prove that a great deal of excellent truth may lie at the bottom of a nation's mind in a condition far from operative. On the whole, however, their belief in the power of truth to produce conduct like itself is far more respectable than the notion, not infrequently ventilated nowadays, that, if only there be sincerity in the heart, it does not much matter what are the doctrines in the mind ; for this amounts to a concession that, if the truth be not found, something else may answer just as well. Knox had a profound belief that, if the truth about God and man were planted in the intellect, it would bring forth fruits of both religion and morality; his aim being to fashion a nation at once loyal towards God and righteous towards man. In his hopes the godward element had the priority; and, therefore, it will be best to begin with the provision which he made for worship.

The practice of extemporaneous prayer in the pulpit is so general in the Presbyterian Churches, and has prevailed so long, that many people are unaware that it does not go back to the beginning. But, at the Reformation, the Scottish Church possessed forms of worship no less than the other Churches which sprang into existence at the same time, and these must have been of special utility in the prevailing scarcity of preachers; because Protestant worship was thereby rendered possible in many places where a regular ministry was not yet procurable. The Book of Common Order was never, indeed, in the strict sense, a liturgy—that is, a prescribed form from which no departure was permissible. On the contrary, it embodied instructions, at sundry places, that the printed prayer should be used, " or another like it "; and at certain places the conductor of the worship was invited to trust to his own inspirations at the moment and to his acquaintance with the circumstances of the case. Thus, its most appropriate name would have been a Directory for Public Worship—the title of the book, compiled by the Westminster divines, by which it was superseded.

It would appear, therefore, that from the first a prayer-book was employed in Scotland more as a help to those of meaner capacity, it being taken for granted that, as competent men were secured, the printed form would be dropped, those who led the devotions of the congregations trusting to their own knowledge of the situation and to the fervour supplied at the moment. And, on the whole, this has been the conception of public worship to which Scotsmen have given their suffrages ever since. The attempt of an English monarch in the seventeenth century to impose an alien form told heavily against a liturgy in the popular mind; and of course during the period of the Covenant the preachers on the moors were not likely to pray by book. The question is, however, an open one, and the Scottish Church is quite entitled, in this as in other matters, to try experiments. Ministers are often deeply dissatisfied with their own attempts at public prayer; and, as culture advances, the lack of form and beauty in extemporaneous utterances will probably be increasingly felt. In all the larger Presbyterian Churches of Scotland efforts have recently been made to supply ministers with aids to public devotion; but the fact that these have proceeded from self-constituted committees and not from the authoritative courts seems to prove that the Church is not yet prepared to move in the matter. It may eventually turn out that the original practice is the one in which the Church of the future will rest—to have forms which may be strictly adhered-to on occasions of special dignity or solemnity, and may be resorted-to by the officiating minister when he is so disposed, but from which departure is not only allowed but recommended, as often as special prayer is called for by novel circumstances or as the tide of devotion flows spontaneously in the preacher's heart.

There is some evidence that the English Book of Common Order, issued in the reign of Edward VI., was occasionally employed in the earliest stages of the Reformation in Scotland; and there is nothing surprising in this taking place at a time when Knox himself was officiating as a minister of the Church of England. For the English congregation of which he was minister at Frankfort, Knox prepared a liturgy, or used one prepared by others; and in his congregation of exiles at Geneva he used this or a modification of it; it being printed with an express intimation that it had obtained the sanction of John Calvin, on whose own order of worship in the same city it was, indeed, modelled. For some years after Knox's final return to his native land this Order of Geneva, as it was called from the circumstance that it had been compiled and used in that city, was adopted in Scotland; and it formed the basis of worship for a long time. In 1564 an enlargement took place, and every minister, exhorter and reader was instructed by the General Assembly to possess himself of a copy and use it in prayers, marriage and administration of the sacraments; and this was frequently issued in subsequent years, with slight modifications.[1]

To the Order of Geneva, when thus published in Scotland, two important appendices were added —Calvin's Catechism and the Psalms of David in metre.

The practice of writing catechisms for the young was general among the Churches of the Reformation, going side by side with the composition of confessions of faith; and the greatest men of the age, like Luther and Calvin, did not disdain to stoop

[1] For full information on all such questions see C. G. McCrie, *Public Worship of Presbyterian Scotland.*

to this humble task ; herein showing their wisdom ; for the influence is incalculable which religious truth exerts on the subsequent life when it has been imprinted on the mind in early years. Luther's Catechism is one of the classics of Germany ; and of Calvin's John Knox expressed the opinion that it was the best which had ever been produced. The Westminster Assembly's Catechism, which displaced that of Calvin, is acknowledged to have been for hundreds of years one of the principal factors in the formation of the Scoto-Irish character, not only in the native homes of the race, but in the new countries which this race has helped to build-up in distant parts of the world. The general aim of all the catechisms of the Reformation was to inscribe on the memory of the young the Creed, the Ten Commandments, and the Lord's Prayer, as embodying the sum of saving knowledge. This arrangement does not appear so palpably on the face of the Westminster Assembly's Catechism ; but the question and answer for which the latter is so famous, " What is man's chief end ? Man's chief end is to glorify God and to enjoy Him for ever," are substantially borrowed from Calvin's Catechism.

The use of singing in public worship was a point on which opinions were divided at the period of the Reformation ; but happily Knox and those who followed him leaned to the positive side, though they only went so far as to place it among the secondary elements of worship. Naturally the Book of Psalms was first turned-to for the materials ; and in the congregation of the refugees at Geneva men of talent were found, among whom the names of Sternhold and Hopkins have survived, to translate the sacred lyrics into singable verse. In the Order of Geneva, as it was issued at Geneva in 1556, fifty-one Psalms appeared, but, after this, the work of translation went on, and the services of new versifiers were secured, among whom William Kethe and John Craig, Knox's colleague in Edinburgh, are deserving of mention, till in the edition, already referred to, of the prayer-book published in 1564 the whole hundred-and-fifty appeared, each with its own fixed tune.

It would be difficult to exaggerate the value of this contribution to Scottish religious life. In every generation since, hundreds of thousands of Scotsmen and their descendants in other countries have practically known the Psalms by heart and thus have had the opportunity of continually tasting the literary charm and extracting the spiritual essence of one of the choicest and most varied of the books of the Bible. In the eighteenth century there were added to the materials of praise, under the name of the Paraphrases, sixty-seven translations from other parts of Scripture ; and in the nineteenth century the use of hymns was introduced on such an extensive scale as to threaten to supersede the Psalms. At present the Church is embarrassed with its riches in the materials of praise ; and measures of compression will no doubt require to be taken in the future ; but a door of entrance will still have to be kept open for the new births of sacred poetical inspiration which time may bring forth. Still the Psalms will not lose their position of preeminence. At the time of the Westminster Assembly the old version was largely superseded by that of Rous ; and this, in its turn, will no doubt have to give place to a better. Praise has of late been securing an increasing proportion of the time spent in public worship, the sermon being thereby shortened ; but it is not to be forgotten that Psalms and Paraphrases are replete with doctrinal instruction ; the hymn-book being sometimes not inaptly called the layman's confession of faith.

It cannot be denied that among the reasons why the Scottish Book of Common Order lost its hold so soon and so completely on the nation, while the English one experienced precisely the opposite fate, must be reckoned its own literary inferiority. It was not composed with the same diligent use of

ancient material, gathered from the liturgies of the
pre-Reformation period ; its spirit is harsh and
denunciatory ; and its language is lacking in music
and felicity. The responses of the congregation are
deliberately excluded ; and many of the prayers
are wearisomely lengthy ; one prayer, for example,
to be used at the Visitation of the Sick, extending
to nearly six pages. On the other hand, there is
embodied in the Baptismal Service a brief sum of
Christian truth which is of rare literary and theological merit ;[1] and there are other materials not a
few to which it will be well to recur when any new directory for public worship is authoritatively undertaken.

One feature on which members of the Church of
England often dwell with fervour in their own
Prayer Book is the Christian Year ; but this is entirely
absent from the Scottish one. In making a clean
sweep of the saints' days of the old Church, Knox
and his coadjutors abolished also the scheme by
which the Church was reminded, by the revolution
of the seasons, of the great events in the life of
the Saviour, such as His Birth, His Passion, His
Resurrection and His Ascension. The motive of
this sacrifice may have been sufficient at the time ;
but it is a question whether now, when the worship
of saints and angels is not likely to come back, this

[1] Quoted in preceding chapter,

loss ought not to be recovered. In the service-books of the Church of Rome there is embodied, not only the Christian Year, but the history of the Christian Church. This is associated with the worship of saints, the notices of whom are full of elements that are legendary and unhistorical. On the other hand, the mind of the ordinary Protestant is nearly a blank as regards the entire period from the year 100 to 1500 A.D. ; and it is well worthy of consideration in what way the examples of martyrs and reformers can be brought to bear on the minds of the people in the worship of the Church. Of the lives of the heroes of religion to the close of the Canon of Scripture worshippers obtain an extraordinary grasp through the public reading of the Old and New Testaments ; many a shepherd on the hill and peasant in her cottage being more familiar with every detail than is the best classical scholar with the literature of Greece and Rome ; but with the history of the twenty centuries created by Christianity the average Presbyterian is woefully ignorant ; and yet these also abound with figures and scenes acquaintance with which would be " profitable for reproof, for correction, for instruction in righteousness, that the man of God may be perfect, throughly furnished unto all good works."

Thus it will be seen that this comparatively

secondary portion of Knox's labours raises many questions the solution of which belongs to the future of our country. But this is characteristic of such a spirit as he was ; and we cannot remind ourselves often enough that the tasks of the Scottish Church are still far from accomplished. They are, indeed, only beginning ; and all forms of belief and practice are subject to modification and development. The supreme standard remains the same ; but it is not a restricting and hampering but an emancipating force. And all arrangements deduced from it are subject to improvement under the teaching of experience and the experiments of time. It would be a poor way of honouring a man who grappled so fearlessly with the problems of his own age and dealt so courageously with the authority of the past to erect him into an oracle from whose utterances it is considered impious to depart ; but it is far more foolish to make the mere negligence of subsequent generations a reason for not attempting to complete the tasks which he initiated but had not time to perfect.

# CHAPTER III,

## THE BOOK OF DISCIPLINE

A S the fruits of the Confession of Faith towards God were provided—for in the Book of Common Order, so were those towards man in the Book of Discipline. As has been already remarked, the latter document originated in the same year as the Confession of Faith—1560—and proceeded from the same authors, who, in their preface, introduce themselves in the following terms :

" To the Great Council of Scotland, now admitted to the regiment by the providence of God, and by the common consent of the estates thereof, your Honours' humble servitors and ministers of Christ Jesus within the same wish grace, mercy and peace from God the Father of our Lord Jesus Christ, with the perpetual increase of the Holy Spirit.

" From your Honours we received a charge dated at Edinburgh, 29 April, in the year of God

1560, requiring and commanding us in the name of the Eternal God, as we will answer in His presence, to commit to writing and in a book to deliver unto your Wisdoms our judgments touching the reformation of religion, which heretofore in this realm, as in others, has been utterly corrupted. Upon the receipt thereof so many of us as were in this town did convene, and in unity of mind do offer unto your Wisdoms these heads subsequent for common order and uniformity to be observed in this realm concerning doctrine, administration of sacraments, election of ministers, provision for their sustentation, ecclesiastical discipline and policy of the Kirk: most humbly requiring your Honours, that, as ye look for participation with Christ Jesus, that neither ye admit anything which God's plain Word shall not approve, neither yet that ye shall reject such ordinances as equity, justice and God's Word do specify: for, as we will not bind your Wisdoms to our judgments further than we be able to prove the same by God's plain Scriptures, so must we most humbly crave of you, even as ye will answer in God's presence, before whom both ye and we must appear to render account of all our deeds, that ye repudiate nothing for pleasure nor affection of men, which ye be not able to improve by God's written and revealed Word."

The treatise thus introduced is in some respects the most remarkable document of that age in Scotland ; and to this day it remains readable in the highest degree, being written with extraordinary vivacity and directness. One would be inclined to say that nothing else bears quite so distinctly the impress of Knox's genius. It comes away in a single gush, and it causes a dazzling image of national prosperity to rise before the mind. Unfortunately it was only an ideal, never destined to be changed into actuality. But for this Knox was not to blame. And ever since it has remained, and it will remain, as a finger pointing forward to possibilities still to be realised. An omission which must strike every reader is the almost total absence of the Presbyterian system of Church government. But for this the conditions were not yet ripe ; and this was amply provided for in the Second Book of Discipline—a monument of the genius of Melville, dating from 1578—which in some minor respects repealed the provisions of this First Book of Discipline, but was in general intended only to expand and confirm its principles.

The Book of Discipline is not a manual of morals, as the Confession of Faith is of doctrine ; although it deals largely with the character and conduct of the members and especially the office-bearers of the Church, as might be gathered from its very name. On discipline proper, in the sense of ecclesiastical censure, it contains two or three chapters ; the contents of which signalise a prominent feature of the order which Knox and his assistants were setting up in Scotland. The ecclesiastical officials were intended to take a very sharp oversight of the morals of the community. " Blasphemy, adultery, murder, perjury, and other crimes capital, worthy of death, ought not properly to fall under the censure of the Church ; because all such open transgressors of God's law ought to be taken away by the civil sword. But drunkenness, excess, be it in apparel or be it in eating or drinking, fornication, oppression of the poor by exactions, deceiving of them in buying or selling by wrong weights or measures, wanton words and licentious living tending to slanders, do properly appertain to the Church of God, to punish the same as God's Word commandeth."

The handling of such offenders by the officials of the Church was to be slow and circumspect, a door of repentance being always left open as long as possible ; but the punishments were intended to be severe in case of obstinacy ; the culminating one being excommunication ; " after which sentence may no person, the wife and family of the culprit only excepted, have any kind of conversation with him ; except it be at the licence and commandment of the ministry for his conversion ; that he, by such mean confounded, seeing himself abhorred of the faithful and godly, may have occasion to repent and so be saved." These arrangements were intended to extend to all ranks and conditions, no respect of persons being allowed : " To discipline must all estates within the realm be subject, if they offend, as well the rulers as they that are ruled ; yea, and the preachers themselves, as well as the poorest within the Church." In another place it is added : " Not only may the life and manners of the ministers come under censure and judgment of the Church, but also of their wives, children and family : judgment must be taken that he neither live riotously nor yet avariciously ; yea, respect must be had how they spend the stipend appointed to their living. If a reasonable stipend be appointed, and they live avariciously, they must be admonished to live so as they receive ; for, as excess and superfluity is not tolerable in a minister, so is avarice and the careful solicitude of money and gear utterly to be condemned in Christ's servants."

In addition to this censureship from other office-bearers, the ministers were to hold a weekly meeting, at which they were to review one another's conduct, under warning that, if they spared from fear or favour to point out one another's faults, they would incur the righteous judgment of God. This idea appears to have been borrowed from the Church of Geneva ; and it suggests that the good men were perhaps a little defective in the sense of humour. With this entire section, indeed, of the Reformers' plans there is connected to the modern mind a suggestion of espionage and disregard of the rights of personality. In practice it has long been curtailed and modified. Yet it is impossible to look at the state of the country at the present time without seeing that we have gone to the opposite extreme in the recognition of the freedom of the subject, and this not to the country's advantage. There is a large class not fit to make a good use of as much personal liberty as is allowed. The members of this class fill our prisons and workhouses at the expense of the public or, if occupying lodgings that are paid for, keep up habits of savage or nomadic life, converting their houses into centres of disease and infection both physical and moral. All who are acquainted with the facts about this class are aware that drastic measures, not unlike those recommended by John Knox, are still required for the protection of society.

It has been suggested that the proper name for

the Book of Discipline would have been the Book of Policy,[1] because its proposals extend far beyond discipline proper to subjects for which "policy" is now the proper term. In the book itself this word appears, however, to be employed in a narrower sense, to denote the external arrangements for the various functions of the Church, such as worship, marriage and the like.[2] Thus, not only was the Sunday to be observed with preaching, the catechising of children and the administration of the sacraments—the Lord's Supper being celebrated four times a year—but on week-days in large towns there was to be daily sermon, or else the reading of Common Prayers with the Scriptures ; and in smaller places at least one week-day service, during which business was to be suspended. The Scripture was to be read in church in order—"that is, that some one book of the Old and the New Testament be begun and orderly read to the end. And the same we judge of preaching, where the minister for the most part remaineth in one place ; for this skipping and divagation from place to place of the Scripture, be it in reading or be it in preaching, we judge not so profitable to edify the Church as the continual following of one text." In private houses the heads

[1] McCRIE, *The Worship of Presbyterian Scotland.*
[2] *History*, ii. 237.

of families were exhorted to use the Common Prayers morning and evening; and, under pain of discipline, they were commanded to instruct the young beneath their roof, in order that these might be fit for admission to the communion; none being considered fit for this ordinance who were not familiar with at least the Lord's Prayer, the Ten Commandments, and the Creed. Marriages were to take place in Church and on Sunday; and young people were not permitted to marry without the consent of their parents, although, if the parents' objections were unreasonable, the young people could appeal to the Church. Burials in Church were not permitted; and there was to be no religious service at funerals—an arrangement considered necessary to counteract the superstitions of Popery, but surely erring itself as far on the opposite side. One interesting service, too soon allowed to fall into desuetude, was the weekly Prophesying, at which all and sundry were encouraged to propound their difficulties or give their comments on the passage selected. This was not unlike a modern American prayer-meeting; and it revealed and developed the spiritual gifts of the laity to the general advantage. " For no man may be permitted to live as best pleaseth him within the Church of God; but every man must be constrained, by fraternal admonition and correction to bestow his labours, when of the Church they are required, to the edification of others." [1]

So much of the Book of Discipline is taken up with the qualifications, the appointment and the functions of the various office-bearers of the Church that these may appear to be its principal topics.

Elders and deacons were to be elected by the free votes of the members, but only for one year, " lest that by long continuance of such officers men presume upon the liberty of the Church. It hurts not that one man be retained in office more years than one, so that he be appointed yearly by common and free election." But deacons could be re-elected only after an interval of three years. The office of the elders consisted in "judging and decerning of causes; in giving of admonition to the licentious liver; in having of respect to the manners and conversation of all men within their charge"; of the deacons "to receive the rents and gather the alms of the Church, to keep and distribute the same. They may assist in judgment with the ministers and elders, and may be admitted to read in the assembly, if they be required and be found able thereto."

Naturally a large amount of space is devoted

[1] *History*, ii. 245.

to ministers. " In a Kirk reformed or tending to reformation none ought to presume either to teach or minister the sacraments till that orderly they be called to the same." Those who presumed to take these functions, especially the latter of them, upon themselves without such qualification were worthy of death.[1] No doubt this severe judgment was aimed first of all at sectaries, like the Anabaptists, but it was extended also to those who had received no licence but that of a corrupt Church : " The papistical priests have neither power nor authority to minister the sacraments of Christ Jesus ; because that in their mouth is not the sermon of exhortation. And, therefore, to them must straight inhibition be made, notwithstanding any usurpation which they have had in that behalf in the time of blindness.    It is neither the clipping of their crowns, the crossing of their fingers, nor the blowing of the dumb dogs called the bishops, neither yet the laying on of their hands, that maketh them true ministers of Christ Jesus.    But the Spirit of God, inwardly first moving the hearts to seek Christ's glory and the profit of His Church, and thereafter the nomination of the people, the examination of the learned and public admission, as before is said, make men lawful ministers of the Word and sacraments.    We

[1] *History*, i. 274.

speak of an ordinary vocation, where Churches are reformed or at least tend to reformation, and not of that which is extraordinary, when God, by Himself and by His only power, raiseth up to the ministry such as best pleaseth His wisdom."

Ample directions are given as to the calling, examining and ordination of ministers. " It appertaineth to the people, and to every several congregation, to elect their own minister." " For altogether this is to be avoided that any man be violently intruded or thrust in upon any congregation." Yet, in the event of the election not being completed in forty days, the authority of the Church could step in and carry out the appointment ; though evidently even in such a case the feelings and wishes of the people were to be considered. The ministers of the neighbourhood were entitled to test the qualifications of the man chosen by the people, and public notice of the proceedings was widely spread, lest anyone should have any complaint to bring against the character of the minister-elect. But, these ordeals being safely passed, he was ordained without laying on of hands—a restriction repealed in the Second Book of Discipline. The appointment was *ad vitam aut culpam*, in the sense not only that the congregation was not at liberty to reject or change the pastor without being able to convict him of crime worthy of deposition, but that he was not at liberty to leave the flock at his pleasure to which he had promised his fidelity and labours.

Ministers of the right stamp were scarce, yet an earnest warning was given against allowing this to interfere with the testing of the qualifications of applicants: "We are not ignorant that the rarity of godly and learned men shall seem to some a just reason why that so straight and sharp examination should not be taken universally; for so it shall appear that the most part of the kirks shall have no minister at all. But let these men understand that the lack of able men shall not excuse us before God, if by our consent unable men be placed over the flock of Christ Jesus, as also that among the Gentiles godly, learned men were also rare as they be now among us when the Apostle gave the same rule to try and examine ministers which we now follow: and last, let them understand that it is alike to have no minister at all and to have an idol in the place of a true minister; yea, and in some cases it is worse; for those that be utterly destitute of ministers will be diligent to search for them; but those that have a vain shadow do commonly without further care content themselves with the same, and so remain they continually deceived, thinking that they have a minister when in very deed they have none. For we cannot judge him a dispenser of God's mysteries that in no wise can break the bread of life to the fainting and hungry souls; neither judge we that the sacraments can be rightly ministered by him in whose mouth God has put no sermon of exhortation."

To meet, however, the difficulties created by the greatness of the field and the paucity of the labourers two extra offices were recognised, neither of which has maintained its place in the Presbyterian system. Of these the first was that of Readers, who were to read prayers and the Scriptures, but were unable to exhort. They were, however, encouraged to attempt a few words of exhortation and instruction; and, if these efforts succeeded, they might look forward to ultimate promotion to the superior office. The other was that of Superintendents. These were to be ten in number, and areas were allotted to them severally, not unlike in extent to the sees of bishops, within which they were to erect the fabric of the Reformed Church, in so far as this had not been already done, and watch over its development where it already existed. They were not only to plant new charges, but to examine the life, diligence and behaviour of ministers, as also the order of their churches and the manners of the people. "They must further consider how the poor be provided; how the youth be instructed; they must admonish where admonition needeth; redress such things as by good counsel they may be able to appease; and, finally, they must note such crimes as be heinous, that by the censure of the Church the same may be corrected."

It is undeniable that such an official bore a close resemblance to a bishop; and it was this that led to the speedy discontinuance of the office. But a superintendent differed essentially from a bishop in this respect, that he was not supposed to belong to a third order above ministers and elders. Besides, the most stringent measures were taken that he should not act like the idle bishops of preceding times, but be a harder worker than any minister; and it was expressly stipulated that he should be liable to the censure of the elders and ministers, who were at liberty to depose him in case of need.

It is not forgotten that a proposal to revive this office was recently made by one of the most eminent ministers of Scotland when preaching before the General Assembly of his Church; his contention being that there are ministers who require superintendence in order to make the most of their talents but, without it, fall into habits

of idleness or vain and aimless energy. The
actual proposal did not take much hold of the
mind of the country; but something was done
in his own denomination towards dealing with
inefficiency; and a widespread impression was produced that in every Church there is requisite an
episcopal function, whether this is to be lodged in
a single person or in such a body as the presbytery.

There is another subject that occupies so much
space in the Book of Discipline that it also might
almost be designated the theme of the whole;
and this is the disposal of the funds accruing
from the disestablishment and disendowment of
the old Church. These were of vast extent,
including the revenues of the abbeys, cloisters,
nunneries, chapels, chantries, cathedral churches,
canonries and the like, which were swept away by
the Reformation. It was the desire of Knox and
his fellow-labourers that these funds should flow into
the treasury of the new Church and be employed
first of all for the support of ministers and superintendents. For these a rate of remuneration is fixed
in the Book of Discipline on a modest scale, but,
as the ministry was no longer to be celibate, a
more liberal allowance than formerly was required.
" Provision must be made not only for their own

sustentation during their lives but also for their wives and children after them. For we consider it a thing most contrarious to reason, godliness and equity, that the widow and children of him who in his life did faithfully serve the Kirk of God and for that cause did not carefully make provision for his family should after his death be left comfortless of all provision." Elders and deacons were not to receive any monetary remuneration.

But the wealth proceeding from the old Church ought far to have exceeded the necessities of the ministry of the new body, on however liberal a scale these had been calculated ; and accordingly Knox and those who shared his ideas were able to contemplate other objects of national importance to which the surplus might be devoted.

One of these was provision for the poor ; and such sentences as the following on this vital subject have not yet lost their virtue : " Every several kirk must provide for the poor within itself ; for fearful and horrible it is that whom not only God the Father in His law, but Jesus Christ in His evangel, and the Holy Spirit speaking by St. Paul hath so earnestly commended to our care, are universally so contemned and despised. We are not patrons for stubborn and idle beggars, who, running from place to place, make a craft of their begging, whom the civil magistrate ought to punish ; but for the widow and fatherless, the aged, impotent or lame, who neither can nor may travail for their sustentation, we say that God commandeth His people to be careful ; and therefore for such, as also for persons of honesty fallen into decay and penury, ought such provision to be made that of our abundance should their indigence be relieved. How this most conveniently and most easily may be done in every city and other parts of this realm, God shall show you wisdom and the means, so that your minds be godly thereto inclined. All must not be suffered to beg that gladly so would do ; neither yet must beggars remain where they choose ; but the stout and strong beggar must be compelled to work, and every person that may not work must be compelled to repair to the place where he or she was born (unless of long continuance they have remained in one place), and there reasonable provision must be made for their sustentation as the Church shall appoint. The order nor sums in our judgments cannot be particularly appointed unto such time as the poor of every city, town or parish be compelled to repair to the places where they were born, or of their residences, where their names and number must be taken and put in roll ; and then may the wisdom of the Kirk appoint stipends accordingly."

16

A further application of these wholesome sentiments is made in the following words to the poor
of another class—those, namely, who, while not
receiving poor relief but paying teinds, were unable,
without a sense of oppression, to sustain the public
burdens they had to bear :—

" We must crave of your Honours, in the name
of the Eternal God and of His Son Christ Jesus,
that ye have respect to your poor brethren, the
labourers and manurers of the ground ; who by
these cruel beasts the papists have been so oppressed
that their life to them has been dolorous and bitter.
If ye will have God author and approver of your
reformation, ye must not follow their footsteps ; but
ye must have compassion on your brethren, appoint-
ing them to pay so reasonable teinds that they may
find some benefit of Christ Jesus now preached unto
them. With the grief of our hearts we hear that
some gentlemen are now as cruel over their tenants
as ever the papists were, requiring of them whatsoever
before they paid to the Church ; so that the papistical tyranny shall only be changed into the tyranny
of the lord or of the laird. We dare not flatter
your Honours, neither yet is it profitable for you
that so we do ; if ye permit such cruelty to be
used, neither shall ye, who by your authority ought
to gainstand such oppression, neither they that use

the same escape God's heavy and fearful judgments. The Gentlemen, Barons, Earls, Lords and others must be content to live upon their just rents, and suffer the Church to be restored to her liberty, that in her restitution the poor, who heretofore by the cruel papists have been spoiled and oppressed, may now receive some comfort and relaxation."

But the principal object on which the surplus was to be expended was education. To every church was to be attached a schoolmaster, able to teach grammar and the Latin tongue, if the town were of any reputation. In landward districts the work might be undertaken by the minister or reader, and the subjects might be more rudimentary, but the thorough teaching of the Catechism must be included. So much for elementary education. Then, in every notable town, and especially in the town of the superintendent, there was to be erected a college or, as we should now term it, a high school, in which the Arts, at least Logic and Rhetoric, together with the tongues, should be read by sufficient masters, for whom honest stipends must be appointed ; and bursaries were to be provided not only for the poor and clever boys of the place, but also for such from the rural districts. This was the second stage— what we now call Intermediate Education—and the summit of the edifice was to be found in the three

universities of St. Andrews, Glasgow and Aberdeen ;
Edinburgh not having yet advanced to the dignity
of a university city.   In St. Andrews there were
three colleges, in Glasgow two, and in Aberdeen two,
with two or more chairs in each.

The Book of Discipline enters minutely into the
arrangements of these great seats of learning,
expatiating on the courses to be taken by the
students and the duties and emoluments of the
professors.   The officials, from principals and rectors
down to porters and beadles, are carefully described,
and the relation of offenders to the civil powers in
the cities where the universities are situated nicely
discriminated.   But here again the essential thing
is the search for talent among the poor and the
provision for free education, while the sons of the
nobility were required to pay according to their
several degrees.

The whole sketch, which is detailed and well-
informed in every direction, is accompanied with a
running comment on the desirability of learning for
its own sake and its utility to the commonwealth ;
and it winds up with the assurance to the nobles, to
whom the Book of Discipline was addressed : " If
God shall grant quietness and give your Wisdoms
grace to set forward letters in the sort prescribed,
ye shall leave wisdom to your posterity, a treasure

more to be esteemed than any earthly treasure you are able to provide for them ! "

This is John Knox's famous scheme for national education. Its outline was clear and imposing ; and the eloquence with which it enforced the claims and advantages of education appealed at once both to the imagination and the common sense of the country. Its accomplishment was delayed and its beneficial results were permanently impoverished by the avarice of the nobility ; but it has never ceased to hold its place as an ideal in the public mind ; and to it must be ascribed in no small degree the reputation for education which Scotland has attained in the world. Even yet, although the sum of human knowledge has increased enormously in extent, the efforts of educationists are absorbed into Knox's scheme without completely filling it up ; and the very latest developments, such as the Education Bill of Lord Young and the munificent gift of Mr. Carnegie, only serve to perfect the ladder which he began to construct.

The entire Book of Discipline may be called Knox's vision of a Scotland religious, virtuous, intelligent and happy ; and, if it be contended that he laid less stress than is due on the last of these adjectives, it may be replied that he in his own

person set an example of happiness, and that a
nation is more likely to come out all right at the
end of this series of adjectives by taking them in
his order than by taking them in the opposite
direction. It was not too proud a boast with
which the Book of Discipline closed when, after
praying the nobles to whom it was addressed to
receive its proposals with an open and favourable
mind, the authors added:—"This our judgment shall
abide to the generations following for a monument
and witness, how lovingly God called you and this
realm to repentance, what counsellers God sent unto
you, and how ye used the same."

# INDEX

ABERDEEN, 63, 89, 244
Adamson, Elizabeth, 12
All-Hallows, London, 34
Alps, 48
Anabaptism, 159, 163, 200, 232
Arminianism, 159
Assembly, General, 65, 76, 81, 109, 131, 167
Assurance, 154
Ayrshire, 15, 44

BALFOUR, JAMES, 29
Balnaves, Henry, 20, 27, 98, 145, 154
Band, The, 54
Bannatyne, Richard, 87, 92, 93
Baptism, 106, 203
Bartholomew, Massacre of St., 88
Beaton, Cardinal, 18, 19, 190
Berwick, 32, 59, 82, 100, 107
Beza, 88
Bible, 17, 46, 55, 91, 93, 129, 198
Book of Common Order, 36, 109, 195, 215, 225
Book of Common Prayer, 33, 39, 40

Book of Discipline, 64, 194, 225
Bothwell, Earls of, 4, 78, 79
Bowes, Marjory, 47
Bowes, Mrs., 46, 100
Brown, Dr. Hume, 26, 27, 110
Buchanan, George, 6, 166
Bullinger, 101, 167

CALDER HOUSE, 43
Calvin, 38, 48, 49, 50, 72, 93, 130, 133, 218
Calvinism, 158, 161-3, 189
Calvin's Catechism, 218, 219
Carlyle, 25, 194
Carnegie, Mr., 245
Castellio, 49, 161
Castle of St. Andrews, 20, 21, 98
Chaplains-in-Ordinary, 33, 34
Church of England, 31-5, 38, 39, 130, 195, 199, 217, 224
Clergy, 11, 19, 42, 55, 61, 62, 123, 124
Confession, Scots, 61, 62, 199
  „      Westminster, 131, 202
Confessions, 146

Congregation, Lords of the, 54, 58, 61, 109, 168, 181
Councils, 201
Craig, John, 178, 220
Cranmer, 31, 103
Craw, Paul, 15
Crossraguel, Abbot of, 108, 125
Cupar Muir, 58

DANTE, 111
Darnley, 77-9, 109
Deacons, 233, 240
" Devout Imaginations," 64
Dieppe, 38, 50, 51, 100, 101, 105, 107
Directory for Public Worship, 216, 222
Discipline, 228
Dundee, 15, 17, 18, 56, 57, 63

EDINBURGH, 11, 12, 18, 42, 43, 45, 53, 60, 63, 75, 79, 82-4, 88, 115, 132, 244
Education, 64, 124, 243
Edward VI., 31, 33, 36, 37, 66, 99, 217
Elders, 233, 240
Election, 157, 164
Elizabeth, Queen, 50, 53, 78, 169-72
England, 28, 31, 35, 53, 58, 59, 80, 100, 101, 103, 105
Erskine of Dun, 12, 43, 63, 74
Excommunication, 109, 228

FAST, GENERAL, 109, 131

Fathers, 201
Feminine attire, 46
France, 20, 25, 27, 51, 53, 58, 60, 66, 67, 70, 84, 88, 182
Francis II., 54, 55, 60, 67
Frankfort, 38-41, 104, 217
Friars, 11, 12, 47, 107, 118

GALLEYS, 25, 27-9
Gardiner, 102
Geneva, 38, 41, 47-50, 53, 106, 107, 161, 162, 230
Geneva Bible, 7, 49
Gifford, 3
Glasgow, 6, 63, 120, 244
Glencairn, Earl of, 44, 90
Goodman, Christopher, 41, 48, 63

HADDINGTON, 3, 4, 6, 18, 20, 58
Hamilton, Patrick, 16, 110
Harlaw, 42
Herkless, 20
*History of the Reformation in Scotland*, 5, 14, 16, 109, 160
Holyrood, 70, 74
Humanism, 6
Huss, 15
Hymns, 221

IDOLATRY, 13, 33, 56, 57, 99, 123, 125, 130, 179, 180
Innes, Mr. Taylor, 109
Irving, Edward, 202

JAMES V., 15, 19, 66

James VI., 79
Justification by faith, 98, 123, 144, 154

KETHE, WILLIAM, 220
Kings, 173, 179, 180, 184
Kirkcaldy of Grange, 20, 83, 84, 90
Knox, Mrs., 11
  „   William, 5

LAING, DR. DAVID, 98
Lamp of Lothian, 4
Lawson, 89, 90
Leith, 15, 58
*Lex Rex*, 178
Lindsay, Sir David, 20, 22, 129
Litany, 39
Liturgy, 215
Lochleven, 71, 80
Lollards of Kyle, 44
Lord's Supper, 35, 45, 55, 74, 99
Luther, 9-11, 14-16, 47, 128, 132, 154, 218

McCRIE, C. G., 218, 231
McCrie, T., 10
Maitland of Lethington, 43, 46, 59, 76-8, 83-6, 168
Major, John, 4, 6
Marriage, 232
Mary of Guise, 20, 44, 50, 54-6, 60, 66, 67, 105, 110, 112, 113, 115, 116, 174, 183, 187

Mary, Queen of Scots, 50, 54, 60, 66-80, 83, 110, 174
Mary Tudor, 33, 37, 40, 42, 50, 53, 100, 102, 107, 108, 179
Mass, 13, 34, 45, 56, 61, 68-70, 72, 74, 99, 100, 105, 108, 124, 179
Melville, Andrew, 227
Melville, James, 86
Ministers, 229, 233
Montrose, 17, 56
Moray, Regent, 43, 69, 72, 78, 80-82, 83
Morton, Earl of, 88, 90, 94
Multitude, "The rascal," 5, 57, 77

NEWCASTLE, 32, 100, 107
Nobility, 16, 64, 65, 72, 76, 80, 107, 168, 174, 184, 186, 245
Non-intrusion, 233

ORDER OF GENEVA, 218, 220
Orders, 32

PARAPHRASES, 221
Paris, 107
Pauperism, 230, 241
Perfectionism, 159
Perth, 56, 63
Philip of Spain, 40, 101
Plato, 69
Poor, The, 64, 124, 240, 244
Pope, The, 23, 61, 78, 103, 122, 124, 185
Portrait, 26

Prayer, 29, 46, 55, 99, 215
Predestination, 49, 108, 157, 162, 189
Priests, 13, 18, 27, 47, 50, 72, 124
Prophesying, 232
Psalms, 134, 218, 220
Puritanism, 40

RANFURLY, 4
Randolph, 58, 60
Readers, 237, 243
Reformation, 14, 31, 35, 42, 50, 54, 55, 61, 110, 197
Rizzio, 78, 190
Rochester, 34
Rous, 221
Row, John, 63, 199
Rutherford, Samuel, 178

ST. ANDREWS, 6, 15, 16, 18, 21, 22, 25, 28, 63, 84, 88, 118, 122, 129, 244
St. Giles, 82, 88, 108, 113
Scone, 57
Servetus, 49, 188
Spain, 73, 102

Spottiswood, 63, 199
Sternhold and Hopkins, 220
Stirling, 56, 58, 80, 82
Superintendents, 237, 238
Synod, Provincial, 42, 55

TITHES, 106
Toleration, 159, 188, 190
Transubstantiation, 123

UNIVERSITIES, 87, 244

WELSH, MRS., 47
Westminster Confession of Faith, 131, 202
Willock, 42, 63, 81, 112, 199
Wishart, George, 16, 17, 19, 20, 23, 26, 29, 43, 110, 112
Women, 50, 69, 107, 167, 168
Wycliffe, 15
Wynram, John, 63, 199

YEAR, CHRISTIAN, 232
Young, Lord, 245

ZWINGLI, 14

*Printed by Hazell, Watson & Viney, Ld., London and Aylesbury.*

*WORKS BY THE SAME AUTHOR*

# IMAGO CHRISTI

## THE EXAMPLE OF JESUS CHRIST

*Crown 8vo, cloth, 5s.*

MR. SPURGEON says :—" This is a delightful book, upon a glorious subject, by one who is better qualified to write it than any other man. With Mr. Stalker's *Life of Christ* we were greatly pleased, and therefore we were prepared to welcome anything from his pen upon a kindred subject. Our highest expectations are exceeded : this is an immortal book."

" The execution is full of ingenuity, and the book can be recommended as a devout and thoughtful commentary on practical Christian life in many phases. Mr. Stalker has broad sympathies and a watchful eye, and speaks in a tone that will commend itself to all his readers."—*Saturday Review.*

" Mr. Stalker certainly proves that the subject is a fruitful one. He shows that the activity of Christ was of a more varied kind than perhaps we are apt to imagine. He exhibits Him in the home, in the State, in society, as a friend, as a worker, as a sufferer, as a philanthropist, as a controversialist, as a man of feeling, and so on ; and on all these subjects he has much that is interesting and much that is instructive to say."—*Scotsman.*

# THE TRIAL AND DEATH OF JESUS CHRIST

## A DEVOTIONAL HISTORY OF OUR LORD'S PASSION

*Crown 8vo, cloth, 5s.*

" The author has a thorough hold of the circumstances and their literature ; his style his admirable in its lucidity and simplicity—enriched several times by felicitous images, as, for instance, on page 11—and his spiritual insight is unerring. No intelligent person can read this book without understanding what happened, and—which is more important—why such things happened. . . . It is a noble book."—Rev. JOHN WATSON in *The British Weekly.*

" Dr. Stalker has given us a book which no one can read without profit. . . . It is probably the best book we have on the subject."—Rev. Professor MARCUS DODS, D.D., in *Expositor.*

" We have here a piece of honest work ably executed. The author has made an earnest and careful study of the passages under review, and of the literature of the subject, and in this way he has qualified himself to write with fulness of knowledge, and, like a preacher of an earlier day, he has ' sought to find out acceptable words.' He has thus produced a book which may be assured of wide popular acceptance, as well as appreciation, amongst those whose studies lie more especially in this direction. It is stimulating as well as instructive in a high degree, and is the production of the competent student not less than the eloquent preacher, and will, like the author's previous productions, take a prominent place among the best popular religious literature of the day."—*Scotsman.*

LONDON : HODDER & STOUGHTON, 27, PATERNOSTER ROW